ROCK RULES!

The Ultimate Rock Band Book

ROCK RULES!

The Ultimate Rock Band Book

By Michèle Rosenthal

SCHOLASTIC INC.
New York Toronto London Auckland Sydney
Mexico City New Delhi Hong Kong

Special thanks to Randi Reisfeld and Ellen Guidone for their help and support on this crazy deadline.

Front Cover (clockwise from top left): Corlouer/A.P.R.F./Shooting Star, Deverill Weekes/Retna Limited, Tom Tavee/Corbis Outline, Steve Sands/Corbis Outline, Michael Schreiber/Retna Limited. Back Cover (top to bottom): Andrew Macpherson/Corbis Outline, Jeff Slocomb/Corbis Outline.

Page 8: Deverill Weekes/Corbis Outline; Page 11: Tara Canova/Retna Limited; Page 15: Jen Lowery/London Features International; Page 19: Kelly Swift/Retna Limited; Page 20: Bill Davilla/Retna Limited; Page 22: C. Patricia Lanza/Shooting Star; Page 24: Laura Luongo/Outline; Page 29: Paul Fenton/Shooting Star; Page 31: David Hum/London Features International; Page 32: John Kelly/Retna Limited; Page 35: Charlie Pizzarello/Retna Limited; Page 36: Steve Jennings/Retna Limited; Page 39: Dennis Kleiman/Retna Limited; Page 41: Bob Mussell/Retna Limited; Page 42: Bill Davilla/Retna Limited; Page 44: John McMurtrie/Retna Limited; Page 47: Mick Hutson/Redferns; Page 51: Melanie Edwards/Retna Limited; Page 53: Bill Davilla/Retna Limited; Page 54: Prager/A.P.R.F./Shooting Star; Page 57: Bill Davilla/Retna Limited; Page 59: Andrew Macpherson/Corbis Outline; Page 63: Paul Fenton/Shooting Star; Page 64: Stephanie Pfriender/Outline; Page 66: Bob Gruen/Star File Photo; Page 69: Micheal Schreiber/Retna Limited; Page 70: Danny Clinch/Outline; Page 72: Bob Berg/Retna Limited; Page 75: Daniel Coston/Retna Limited; Page 76: John Popplewell/Retna Limited; Page 78: Steve Jennings/Retna Limited; Page 80: Paul Natkin/Outline; Page 82: M.B. Charles/Retna Limited; Page 85: Yael/Retna Limited; Page 87: M.B. Charles/Retna Limited; Page 90: Danny Clinch/Corbis Outline; Page 92: Jay Blakesberg/Retna Limited; Page 95: John Kelly/Retna Limited.

ISBN 0-439-24380-7

Cover and interior design by Louise Bova

Copyright © 2000 Scholastic Inc.

All rights reserved. Published by Scholastic Inc.

12 11 10 9 8 7 6 5 4 3 2   0 1 2 3 4 5 6/0

Printed in the U.S.A.

First Scholastic printing, November 2000

Table of Contents

INTRODUCTION

Call it pop, soul, hip-hop or funk, rap, ska, swing, be-bop or punk — as Billy Joel once famously sang, *"It's still rock 'n' roll to me."* And no matter how you sing it, mosh to it, dance to it, relate to it, brood-if-you're-in-the-mood to it, **rock** is what totally **rules**!

Behind the music, of course, are the artists. They're musicians, singers, songwriters, performers — and in many cases, superstars. The charts are burning up with their success stories from all over the country. From the fertile music scene of Los Angeles to the blistering heat of Florida, rock bands cover the United States and bring their own unique creativity to the airwaves.

You dig listening to their music, now you'll love hearing the stories of how the bands were put together, how they got their recording contracts, what songs made them famous, and what inspires their creativity. Plus, find out the scoop on every album, and then, how you can get in touch with your favorite bands.

It's time to plug in your amp, pump up the volume, crank out some tunes, and get ready to rock and roll, 'cause the bands you're about to meet prove without a doubt — rock rules!

1. They had to be *TRL* worthy: That is, not so much in constant rotation on that MTV show, but they had to have a major degree of popularity. Translation: Most people you know have to have heard of them!

2. They had to be original, fresh, and fly; no copycats need apply. In other words, they had to be musical risk takers, even pioneers, and not settle for just giving fans the "same old, same old."

3. They had to be interesting, unpredictable, and, as another rock pioneer once wrote, "simply irresistible"!

NOW, WHO ARE THEY?

Blink-182, Limp Bizkit, KoRn, and Red Hot Chili Peppers — the bands who've blasted radios with various and new forms of punk rock. Plus, Smash Mouth and No Doubt who've each proved there's more to ska than its original beat. Then there's the combo of Carlos Santana and Rob Thomas, the two guys who put a new pop groove in Latin rock. The Dave Matthews Band, who blended jazz with some funk. And don't forget Kid Rock and Everlast who both mixed some rock into the world of hip-hop.

TOM DeLONGE

MARK HOPPus

TRAVIS BARKER

HURLEY IN

CHAPTER 1

BLINK-182

BIGGest Hits:

* "What's My Age Again?"
* "All the Small Things"
* "Adam's Song"

HOW THE BAND GOT ITS NAME: Originally the boys decided on the name Blink, but when another band threatened to sue because they had the same name, Mark, Tom, and Travis decided to add the number 182. They picked the number randomly and it has no meaning.

CITY OF ORIGIN: San Diego, California
STYLE OF MUSIC: punk rock, pop punk
MUSICAL INFLUENCES: Various punk rock bands
OFFICIAL WEBSITE: www.blink182.com

CONTACT THE BAND:

Blink-182
c/o MCA Records
70 Universal Plaza
Universal City, CA 91608

Discography:

* Enema of the State (1999)
* Dude Ranch (1997)
* Cheshire Cat (1995)
* Buddha (1994)
* Fly Swatter (1993)

THE BOYS IN THE BAND:

Name: Thomas Matthew DeLonge
Birth date: December 13, 1975
Birthplace: San Diego, California
Musical instrument: vocals, guitar

RANDOM FACTS:

* Tom believes in aliens
* Before the band took off, Tom used to work at Gary's Chicken and Ribs in Poway, CA, and also used to drive a truck to deliver cement piping
* Tom played a small role in the movie *Idle Hands*
* Tom's favorite music is hip-hop
* Tom started skateboarding in the third grade

QUOTABLE QUOTE:

* Tom recalls the initial jam session he had with Mark: "It sounds stupid, but the first time we sat down and played together, it was just magical."

Name: Mark Allen Hoppus
Birth date: March 15, 1972
Birthplace: Ridgecrest, California
Musical instrument: guitar
Dues paying gig: Wherehouse record store clerk

RANDOM FACTS:

* Mark was inspired to write the song "Going Away to College" on Valentine's Day after seeing the movie *Can't Hardly Wait*
* Mark's hero is TV's Homer Simpson
* Mark travels with a stuffed bunny given to him by his girlfriend
* Mark makes a cameo appearance in Fenix*TX's video *All My Fault*

* Mark's favorite music is by the band Jimmy Eat World
* Mark's dad was a hi-tech weapons engineer

QUOTABLE QUOTES:

* To explain the band's sense of humor, Mark says: "I think we never finished developing after high school. We finished high school, and we started the band, and we've been in the band ever since. It's like suspended animation."

* "The biggest compliment of all is a kid saying we opened up his or her eyes to a new style of music."

Name: Travis Landon Barker
Birth date: November 14, 1975
Birthplace: Riverside, California
Musical instrument: drums

RANDOM FACTS:

* Travis collects Cadillacs and old bicycles
* Travis runs Famous Stars and Straps, a belt and belt buckle company
* Travis has between forty and fifty tattoos, including a beat box on his stomach and a tribute to his mother on his arm
* Travis' favorite music is King Diamond
* Travis loves leopard prints. He has a cowboy hat (the same one he wore in the *All the Small Things* video) and recliner chair in the animal pattern

mArk HopPus

QUOTABLE QUOTE:

✳ "I've never been one to party on tour. When all the other bands are going out after the show, I'm sitting in a room practicing. I feel guilty if I don't, like I'm taking everything for granted."

RANDOM FACTS:

✳ All three band members appeared in the 1999 movie *American Pie*

✳ Mark and Tom founded a website so fans could buy the same kinds of clothes they wear; the website is called www.loserkids.com

✳ Mark and Tom have written a screenplay (*Snipe Hunting*) for a film they plan to produce

✳ Other names considered before they settled on *Enema of the State: Turn Your Head and Cough, Viking Wizard Eyes, Blink-182: Electric Boogaloo*

The guys' favorite shoes:

✳ Mark: Pumas
✳ Tom: Converse All Stars
✳ Travis: Pumas

The guys' favorite companion:

✳ Mark: his CD player
✳ Tom: his little AM radio
✳ Travis: his best friend, Tim Millhouse

The guys' favorite TV show:

✳ Mark: *The Simpsons*
✳ Tom: *The X-Files*
✳ Travis: Doesn't watch TV

THE BLINK-182 STORY

They're called the "stepchildren of punk rock," the outrageous younger siblings who give the rest of the family a bad name, the bad boys of the West Coast. They are Blink-182, a three man band who hit stardom by singing songs about breakups and loneliness — and by — okay — running around naked onstage and in videos. That last bit started as an in-band joke and will not be seen onstage in the future. "We're kind of sick of it now," says Blink's lead singer, Mark Hoppus. It doesn't seem to matter *what* this band does though, fans love them.

Coming out of San Diego, California, at the height of the punk scene, Blink-182 are best known for their rockin' tunes, unusual stage attire, *and* their sense of humor. But don't laugh, this band also has a serious side. Says lead singer Mark Hoppus, "I think we get pigeonholed as a joke band, but none of our songs are joke songs. 'What's My Age Again' is kind of lighthearted . . . about staying young and acting infantile. But the songs themselves are serious songs about girls, love, life, and problems." Although their behavior and unexpected antics may seem funny and disrespectful at times, this band and the guys in it are no joke.

WHO ARE THESE GUYS ANYWAY?

The core of Blink has been together since 1992. Lead singer Mark Hoppus moved to San Diego from the East Coast to attend college; he wanted to be an English teacher. But after five years of school he decided to drop out and start a band. He had been playing guitar since he was in high school when his dad bought him his first six-string. His dad recalls, "He helped me paint a house . . . so I bought him a bass guitar and an amp. [Mark] started a garage band, and all the neighborhood kids would line up outside, sit on this brick wall, and listen." Lucky for Mark, by the time he decided to start a new band he had already met his future bandmate, guitarist Tom DeLonge.

When Mark and Tom met, Tom was only fourteen years old and

was hanging out with Mark's sister. Mark and Tom's musical chemistry was immediate. For a month they jammed together and wrote some songs before they recruited one of Tom's friends, drummer Scott Raynor, to join them.

HOW THE BAND WORKS

Mark and Tom share all singing and songwriting duties and they insist that the band is totally fair to each member. "Our band is totally run by democracy," explains Mark. "Everyone has a say and we try to respect one another." The band's initial goal was to play in public and they started doing that pretty quickly. By 1993 they felt ready to record and self-released their first EP, *Fly Swatter*.

While playing in the local nightspot scene Blink struck up a friendship with another San Diego band, The Vandals, whose tiny label Kung Fu agreed to take on Blink. Kung Fu released Blink's second album, *Buddha*, in 1994. The growing exposure of the band then brought them to the attention of a larger label, Cargo Records, who signed Blink to a one-album deal. The result of the deal was the release of Blink's third album in 1995. According to Mark, they called the album *Cheshire Cat* because Mark "love[s] the story of Alice in Wonderland, and especially the character of the Cheshire Cat, and [he] thought that since [Blink] has such a [weird] sense of humor, [the name] just fit."

A lot of Blink's popularity is due to their live shows. Kids loved to see the band perform so much that the word of mouth spread quickly and made Blink a hot band to catch — which made them a hot band for record companies to sign.

GOING TO THE MAJORS

In 1996 Blink inked a major label deal with MCA Records and a year later released their fourth album, *Dude Ranch*. Suddenly, Blink was taking the world by storm as the song "Dammit" became a huge success. They had a large following in Canada and the United States, but in Australia, Blink's popularity was off the charts; *Dude Ranch* went platinum, selling over ten million copies.

While parents don't approve of the language in Blink's lyrics, kids have made these three guys superstars. But just as their careers were skyrocketing, Scott decided to leave the band. Suddenly Blink was missing a drummer. Luckily, they found a replacement in Travis Barker, the drummer for the Aquabats, another local band.

Of the three band members, Travis is quietest, and the most musically schooled. His mother started him playing drums when he was four and he is now a skilled musician with training in everything from jazz to madrigals. In fact, it was Travis's mother who encouraged him to pursue a career in music. Tragically, the day before he started high school, she died of cancer. Before she passed away however, Travis' mom told him, "I just want you to play the

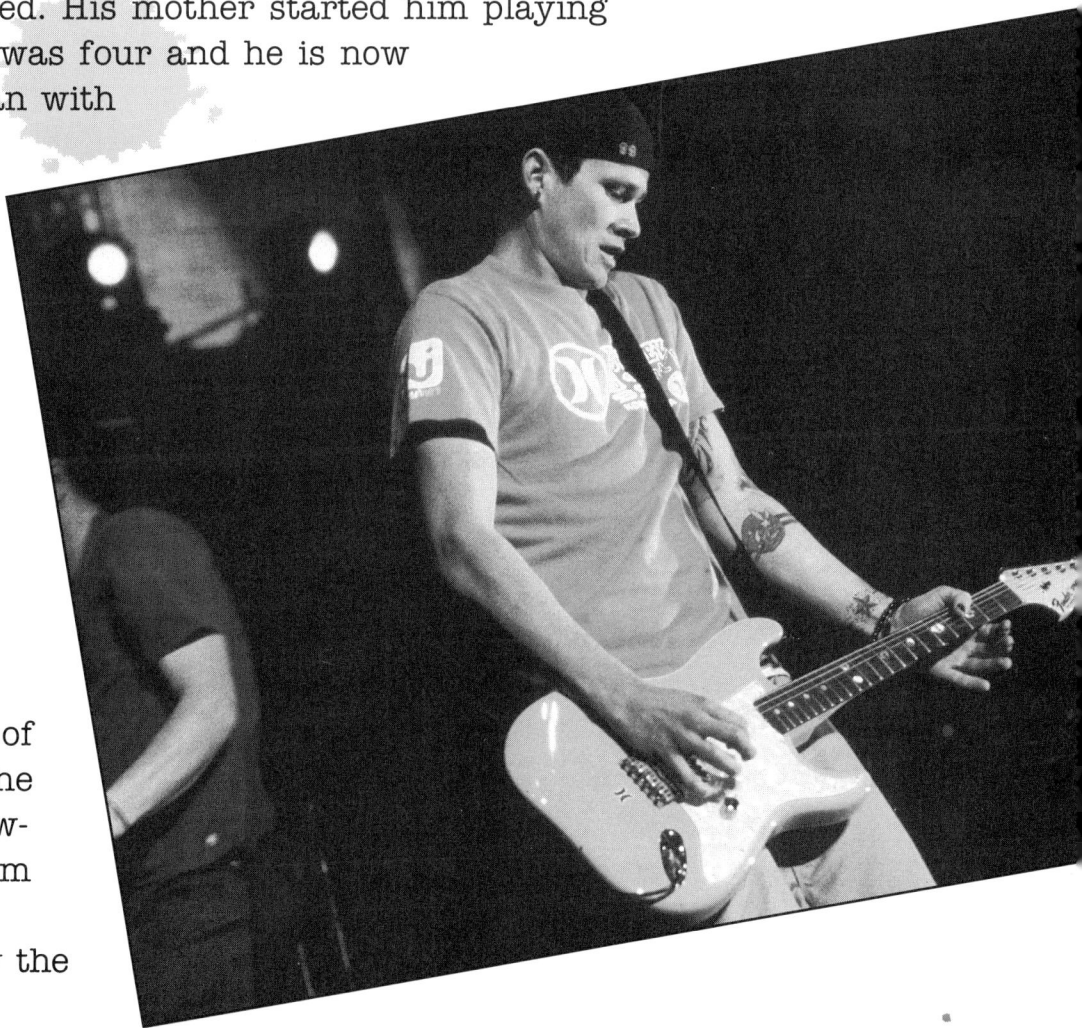

drums and be happy." Travis took her advice and still plans to go to music school.

Together the new trio recorded Blink's fourth album, *Enema of the State,* which was released in 1999. It became an even bigger hit than the last album. Fans loved the songs and funny videos for "What's My Age Again" and "All the Small Things." And they also got into more serious tunes like "Adam's Song," which Mark explains is "about me being lonely on tour and thinking that I was never going to be able to find a girl to love." Tom adds that the song is inspirational. He says, "The whole song's about there being something better out there." That sure was true for Blink-182. The success of *Enema of the State* guaranteed the band permanent punk status.

Kids loved to see the band perform so much that word of mouth spread quickly and made Blink a hot band to catch.

Next up for Blink in 2001: a live album that includes some of the material from *Enema of the State,* plus some of the band's classic tunes from their earlier releases. The show that was actually captured on tape was one they performed at an amphitheater in Los Angeles. Most of 2000 the band kept busy on a worldwide tour to support the new album. About the tour Mark said, "We're all [very excited] about it. This is the dream tour everybody wishes they could do." But it wasn't quite smooth sailing. Midway through the tour Travis broke his pinky and had to take a break from the band. These guys are such pros they didn't stop the tour, they just got a friend to sit in on drums and let the show go on!

CHAPTER 2

No Doubt

HOW THE BAND GOT ITS NAME: The band's name comes from John Spence, one of the founding members: "No doubt" was his favorite expression.

CITY OF ORIGIN: Orange County, California

STYLE OF MUSIC: ska/pop

OFFICIAL WEBSITE: www.nodoubt.com

Biggest Hits:

* "Simple Kind of Life"
* "Just a Girl"
* "Spiderwebs"
* "Ex-Girlfriend"
* "Don't Speak"

AWARDS/NOMINATIONS:

* Nominated for Best Rock Album and Best New Artist at the Grammy Awards (1997)

* Nominated for Favorite New Artist Pop/Rock at the American Music Awards (1997)

* Awarded Best Group Video at MTV Music Awards (1997)

* Awarded Outstanding Female Vocalist Statewide and Outstanding Group Statewide at the California Music Awards (1998)

* No Doubt was nominated for Most Stylish Video; Gwen was nominated for Most Fashionable Female Artist at the VH1/Vogue Fashion Awards (1999)

* At the VH1/Vogue Fashion Awards No Doubt won the award for Most Stylish Video for the song "New" (1999)

Discography:

* Return of Saturn (2000)
* Tragic Kingdom (1995)
* Beacon Street Collection (1995)
* No Doubt (1992)

CONTACT THE BAND:

P.O. Box 8899, Anaheim, CA 92812

RANDOM FACTS:

* Much of the motivation behind the music on *Return of Saturn* was based on the band, and mostly Gwen, figuring out who they were over the past couple of years

* No Doubt has been together for ten years

THE BOYS (AND GIRL) IN THE BAND:

Name: Gwen Stefani
Birth date: October 3, 1969
Birthplace: Fullerton, California
Musical influences: movie soundtracks including *The Sound of Music*, *The Muppet Movie*, and *Annie*, plus the bands Madness, The Selecter, *The Untouchables*, and Fishbone
Musical instruments: vocals — she's the lead singer
Family: Gwen is so super close to her parents, brothers Tony and Dennis, and sister Jill that she lives at home
Dues paying gigs: sales clerk in a department store, Dairy Queen server

RANDOM FACTS:

* Gwen cowrote all of the tracks on *Return of Saturn* and penned two of the tracks on her own

* Girls who dress to imitate Gwen's fashion style are called "Gwenabees"

* Gwen is dating the lead singer of Bush, Gavin Rossdale. They met when the two bands toured together

* Before joining No Doubt and while they recorded *Tragic Kingdom* Gwen was an art major at Cal State Fullerton College

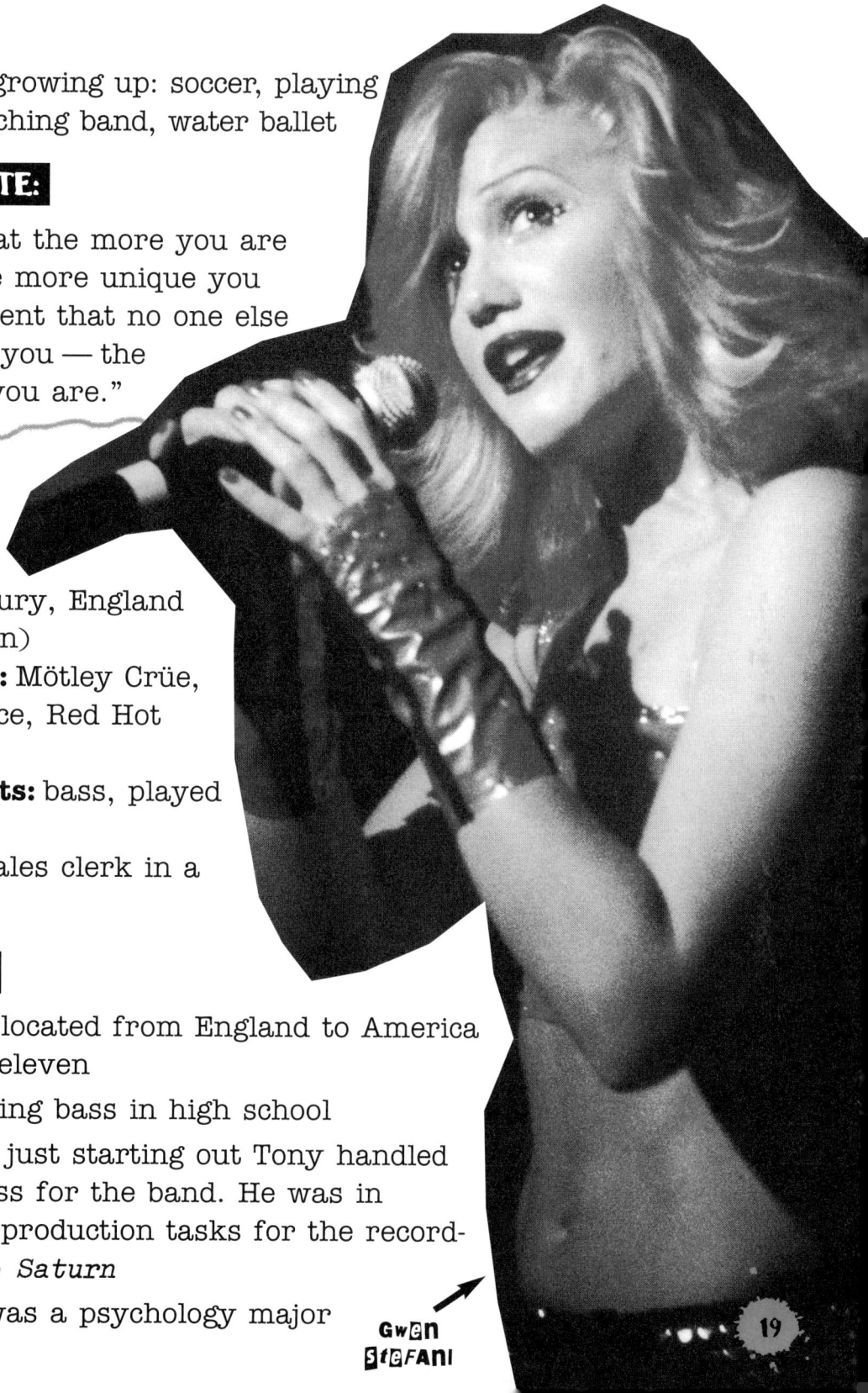

* Gwen's hobbies growing up: soccer, playing piccolo in a marching band, water ballet

QUOTABLE QUOTE:

* "I've learned that the more you are yourself and the more unique you are — to the extent that no one else is anything like you — the more powerful you are."

Name: Tony Kanal
Birth date: August 27, 1970
Birthplace: Kingsbury, England (a suburb of London)
Musical influences: Mötley Crüe, Duran Duran, Prince, Red Hot Chili Peppers
Musical instruments: bass, played sax in high school
Dues paying gigs: sales clerk in a department store

RANDOM FACTS:

* Tony's family relocated from England to America when Tony was eleven

* Tony began playing bass in high school

* When they were just starting out Tony handled all of the business for the band. He was in charge of all preproduction tasks for the recording of *Return to Saturn*

* In school Tony was a psychology major

Gwen Stefani

There's no doubt about this foursome: they rock!

Adrian Young, Gwen, Tom Dumont, Tony Kanal

QUOTABLE QUOTES:

* About the band's place in the music scene, Tony says: "Maybe we fit in between extremes. We didn't fit [when we released the last album] either and it turned out to be a good thing. We can fill a void."

* "You just make the best record you can and hope it finds its place."

Name: Adrian Young
Birth date: August 26, 1969
Birthplace: Long Beach, California
Musical influences: The Doors, Jimi Hendrix
Musical instruments: drums

RANDOM FACTS:

* In addition to being a great drummer, Adrian is also a pro at golf

* Adrian has been playing drums since Christmas day 1987

* In school Adrian was a psychology major

* Adrian proposed marriage — and his girlfriend, Nina, accepted — onstage during a No Doubt show at The Fillmore in San Francisco

QUOTABLE QUOTE:

* About fan response to the band's latest album, *Return of Saturn*, Adrian says, "Some people are gonna love it, and some people are gonna hate it, but the one thing that I'm really proud of is that it definitely stands out. We have an original sound unlike other groups out now. Whether [it's bad] or it's good, it's definitely No Doubt."

Name: Tom Dumont
Birth date: January 11, 1968
Birthplace: Los Angeles, California
Musical influences: Alex Lifeson (Rush), Ritchie Blackmore (Deep Purple), Oingo Boingo
Musical instruments: guitar

RANDOM FACTS:

* Tom has been playing guitar for more than half his life
* Tom's hobbies are surfing, home decorating, and collecting old radios
* Before he joined No Doubt Tom was playing in his sister's heavy metal band called Rising
* While in school Tom was a music major

QUOTABLE QUOTE:

* "There's one song on [*Return of Saturn*] that really stands out to me as different — and the most No Doubt song — and that's 'Bath Water.' It started out spontaneously with Tony playing this really simple bass line with a groove to it. Gwen started singing words to it and forty minutes later we had a song, a really fun song."

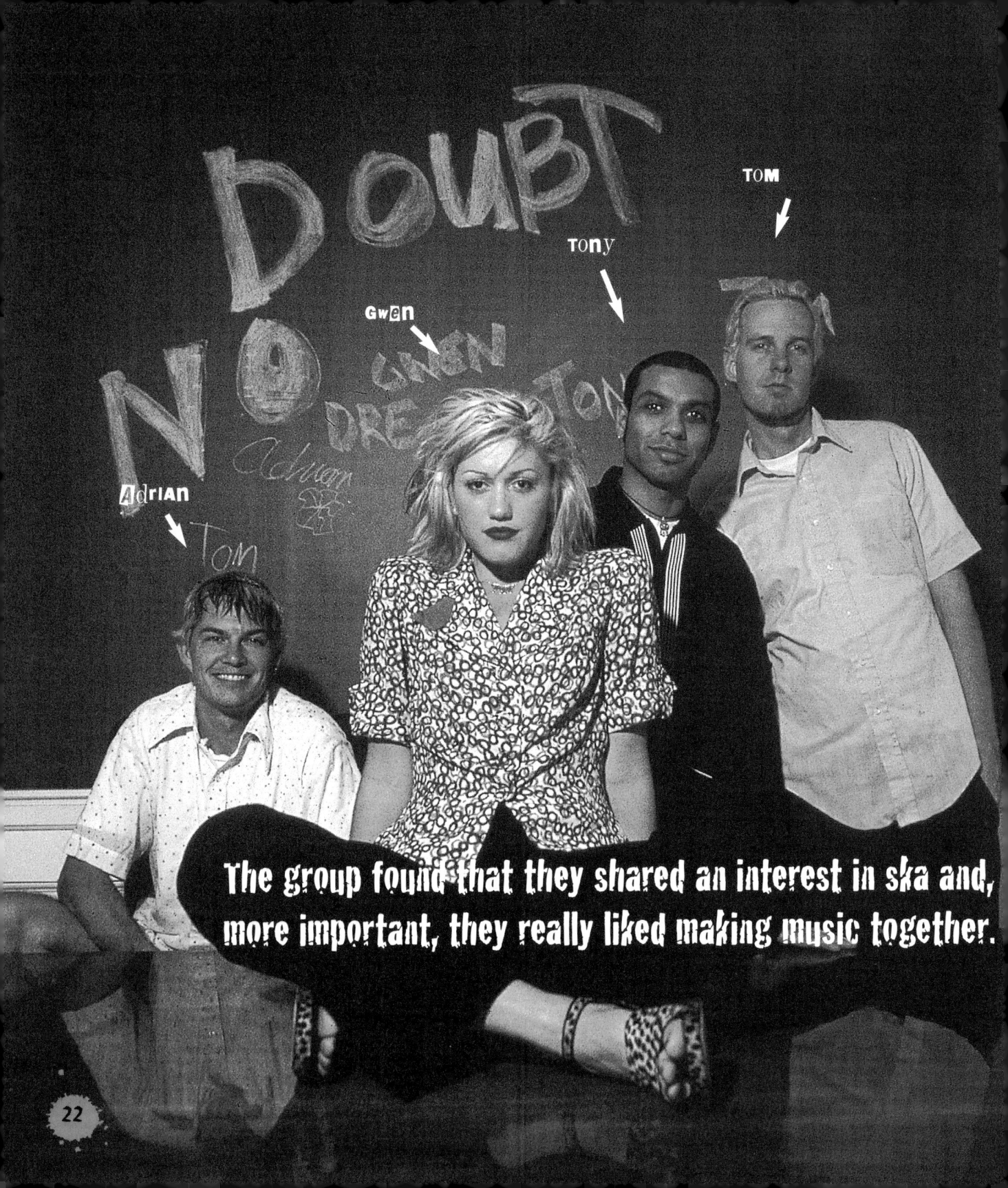

DOUBT NO

Gwen

Adrian

tony

TOM

The group found that they shared an interest in ska and, more important, they really liked making music together.

THE NO DOUBT STORY

While there are many boy bands touring the country and winning fans with hip-hop, rap, and outrageous lyrics, there is another band, fronted by a *girl*, making tracks to the top of the charts with a different sort of beat. The band is called No Doubt and their rhythm is ska, a style that combines rock 'n' roll with a Jamaican island sound. It was a style that just happened to be very popular in England in the eighties at about the same time No Doubt got together.

A BROTHER + A SISTER + A FRIEND = A BAND

In 1986 Eric Stefani and his high school buddy John Spence decided to form a band. John liked to sing and Eric, who played keyboards, had been writing songs since he was a little kid. He used to ask his younger sister Gwen to sing the songs he wrote. That was fine with her, since Eric and Gwen were best friends. Gwen liked to tag along to rehearsals. One day Eric convinced her to sing with John. It was all very casual, but something cool happened that day. The trio found that they shared an interest in ska and, more important, they really liked making music together. It was that simple. No Doubt was born.

The band soon began appearing on the local Orange County/Anaheim scene. They played at several parties before they got their first real gig at Fender's Ballroom in Long Beach, California; No Doubt was second on a bill of fourteen other bands. Tony Kanal, a high school junior, was in the audience for the show and went to meet the band after the performance. Soon after, No Doubt held auditions for a bassist and Tony showed up. He won the job. He also won Gwen's heart. The two ultimately started dating and were together for seven years.

The band started to groove together. They won a loyal fan base by the end of 1987. Then, tragedy struck. John Spence unfortunately decided to take his own life, and the band was shattered. They considered breaking up, but eventually decided that John would want them to go on.

Gwen became the sole vocalist for the group and in time, No Doubt added guitarist Tom Dumont (who'd just left a heavy metal band and responded to a No Doubt ad, looking for a guitar player). They also brought drummer Adrian Young on. Now the band was solid. They expanded their sound to include the personal style of each member. In 1991, as a result of their local fan exposure and the demo tapes they passed around, they were awarded their first recording contract.

A LITTLE DOUBT

No Doubt's first self-titled album was done on a tiny budget. It had fourteen tracks and the band recorded them in between working and going to school. Unfortunately, the album was released in 1992 — the popular sound at the time was called grunge. Bands like Nirvana and Soundgarden hogged the airwaves. No one was very interested in No Doubt's more upbeat sound. One radio promoter told the band, "It would take an act of God for [you] to get on the radio." Despite the less than enthusiastic reception the album got, No Doubt went on a two-week thirteen show tour to support it. They played only on the West Coast, at first, but later did small clubs all over the United States.

While touring was a great experience, it didn't help sell the album. In 1993, the band began working on a new one. It would be called *Beacon Street Collection*, named after the the house in Anaheim, California, where some of the bandmembers were living, and the garage studio in which several of the tracks were recorded.

Because their record company had lost a little faith in the band and was not being very supportive, No Doubt self-released the album and sold out of the first thousand CDs within two weeks by selling them at shows and local record stores.

No Doubt hit a rough patch while they finished their third album, *Tragic Kingdom.* It was recorded in eleven different studios over two and a half years — but it was not an easy time for the band. First, Eric decided to quit (he is now one of the animators for *The Simpsons*). Second, Tony broke up with Gwen. All that tension and pain might have split up a less determined band, but the quartet managed to stay together. Gwen put her energy and emotions into writing and the album ended up containing No Doubt's breakout hit, "Don't Speak."

Released in the fall of 1995, *Tragic Kingdom* was a mixture of ska, new wave, pop, punk, and rock. The first single off the album, "Just a Girl," eventually hit number ten on the charts. "That single surprised . . . me," says Tom Dumont who wrote the music. "I always thought the song was cool, but I never expected it to fly like it [did]." The video for the song was all over MTV — finally No Doubt's career really took off. Another single, "Spiderwebs," was picked up by MTV's *Buzz Bin*, and "Don't Speak" eventually went all the way to number one on the charts. *Tragic Kingdom* wasn't so tragic after all: Eventually the album went platinum and now has sold over fifteen million copies. The question then became, could they do that again?

OUTER SPACE

To promote the success of *Tragic Kingdom* No Doubt hit the road for twenty-seven grueling months. By the time they came home from an extensive international tour they were exhausted — and not feeling particularly creative. "I think I lost bits of myself when I was on tour," admits Gwen. "I spent the last couple of years trying to find what was the real me, the real Gwen." *Return of Saturn,* the band's follow-up album, became a tribute to that self-exploration.

No Doubt had written *nothing* on the road. Back home in California they began to work slowly, in small groups, recording tracks on a tiny tape recorder. "We got together and decided that rather than repeat *Tragic Kingdom,* we should have a goal — to improve as songwriters. To stretch," explains guitarist Tom. And that's just what they did. For this album the band relied on no outsiders for help; they penned all the tracks themselves. After two years of hard work they completed *Return of Saturn,* a fourteen song collection that spans many different styles of music from punk, to hip-hop to world beat to symphonic rock, while telling a coming-of-age story about Gwen herself.

The title of the album has a specific meaning. It comes from a scientific truth about the planet Saturn: It takes Saturn twenty-nine years to orbit the sun. The idea then is that it takes a person twenty-nine years to live long enough to come full circle and figure out who you really are and what your place is in the world.

Gwen sums it up this way, "[I was thinking] who am I, and how did I get to this point in my life, when I thought I was going to be something completely different? . . . The truth is, I feel like I've been turned inside-out after writing this album. It's everything that I have been in the last two years, which have been really hard years for me." The songs on *Return of Saturn* "Marry Me," "Simple Kind of Life," and "Ex Girlfriend" tell Gwen's story as she turned thirty.

No Doubt's sound today includes a much broader base of styles than their earlier albums. They can no longer be solely labeled a ska band, although you can still hear that in their work. Tony admits, "It's really hard to pigeonhole us now. In the past people have thrown us in the ska or new wave [category], trying to put different labels on us . . . But as far as I'm concerned, I think we're just a true American rock band." He's right. *Return of Saturn* was an instant hit with both fans and critics. It's been a tough trip from the kingdom to Saturn, but No Doubt definitely has come full circle as they head up the charts again.

CHAPTER 3

LIMP BIZKIT

BIGGest Hits:

* "Rearranged"
* "Counterfeit Down"
* "Break Stuff"

HOW THEY GOT THEIR NAME: According to lead singer Fred Durst the band chose the name "because it was the stupidest name we could think of."

COOLEST THING THEY'VE DONE: Summer 2000 *free* concert tour. Says Fred Durst, "We're going to give back to our fans what they've given us."

CITY OF ORIGIN: Jacksonville, Florida

STYLE OF MUSIC: fusion of metal, punk, and hip-hop = rapcore

OFFICIAL WEBSITE: www.bizkitweb.com

CONTACT:

* Limp Bizkit, c/o Interscope Records, 825 8th Avenue, 29th Floor, NYC 10019
* Fred Durst Unsigned Band Search, 9000 Sunset Boulevard, Suite 525, Los Angeles, CA 90069
* Limp Bizkit, P.O. Box 93655, Los Angeles, CA 90093-998

Discography:

* Chocolate Starfish and the Hotdog Flavored Water (2000)
* Significant Other (1999)
* Three Dollar Bill Y'all (1998)

THE BOYS IN THE BAND:

Name: Fred Durst
Birth date: August 20, 1971
Birthplace: Gastonia, North Carolina
Musical influences: Kiss, Blondie, Wu Tang
Musical instruments: mostly Fred sings, but he can also play guitar, drums, and bass
Family: Fred has a daughter, Adriana
Dues paying gigs: surf shop manager, skate park attendant, artist, tattoo artist, coffeehouse bartender, landscape artist

RANDOM FACTS:

* Fred directed Limp Bizkit's video for "Faith"
* Fred has been a guest artist on records from such bands as KoRn, Videodrone, and Soulfly
* Fred is working on a movie script. Fred would like to become a film director
* Fred's English bulldog is named Bizkit
* In 1999 Fred bought a house in Los Angeles
* Fred's mother's voice is on the *Significant Other* album
* Fred served eighteen months in the Navy

QUOTABLE QUOTES:

* "[Limp Bizkit] is like a six-dimensional thing. We layer on everything — rap, metal, alt rock. It's just like we have different layers for different moods and tones and feelings. We just have this balance."
* "I want to put great music in the world. When you become successful, people listen to you, and you have more of a chance to keep doing things that are gonna leave good marks behind. That's what I'm doing."

Name: Sam Rivers
Musical instrument: bass
Musical influences: grunge, old rock
Dues paying gigs: worked at a fast food restaurant in a mall in Jacksonville, Florida
Family: Sam is married to his junior high school sweetheart, WWF owner Vince McMahon's daughter Stephanie (a.k.a. Roxie); they have a son named Gaige
Currently resides in: Mesa, Arizona

Fred

RANDOM FACTS:

* Born in 1978, Sam is the youngest member of Limp Bizkit; he was only nineteen when *Three Dollar Bill Y'all* was released

* Sam has two tattoos for his wife Roxie: one is on his right wrist: an "R"; the other is on his right ankle: the word "Roxie" with a design around it

* Sam trained for one year in a wrestling school. He often goes to wrestling shows with his wife and sometimes gets on the mic to announce an event

* Sam has been playing guitar since he was fifteen

* Sam has had orange, pink, brown, and blond hair

* Sam proposed to Roxie onstage at a Limp Bizkit show in November 1999

29

Name: Wes Borland
Birth date: February 7, 1975
Birthplace: Nashville, Tennessee
Musical instrument: guitar; he started playing at the age of twelve (blues, country, fingerpicking) because his parents wouldn't let him get a drum set
Musical influences: David Bowie, Ice Cube
Dues paying gigs: coffeehouse bartender
Family: wife, Heather McMillan

RANDOM FACTS:

* Wes is working on a solo album, *Ruining the Miracle,* which will be released soon

* Wes quit smoking on February 9, 1999

* Wes drives a 1999 Toyota Pickup truck

* Wes almost dropped out of Limp Bizkit because of his acceptance to art school. He drew the covers for *Three Dollar Bill Y'all* and *Significant Other*

* Wes designs and sews all of the costumes he wears for Limp Bizkit shows

* Wes was an art student at Anderson School of the Arts in Jacksonville, Florida

QUOTABLE QUOTE:

* About the album title, *Significant Other,* Wes says: "The title refers to male-female relationships, of course. But it also refers to this record as our 'significant other.' [It] is the record that we've wanted to make since we started this band."

Name: John Everett Otto
Musical instrument: drums
Previous bandmember of: a jazz band

RANDOM FACTS:

* John was a student at Anderson School of the Arts in Jacksonville, Florida, when he was drafted into the band
* John was studying jazz
* John began playing drums at the age of seventeen
* John likes to play paintball

Name: Leor Dimant; aka DJ Lethal
Musical instrument: turntables (sound manipulator)

RANDOM FACTS:

* Lethal used to be a member of House of Pain
* He is working on a solo project that will feature members of many other bands
* Lethal produced Sugar Ray's debut album, *Lemonade and Brownies*
* Lethal is originally from Latvia

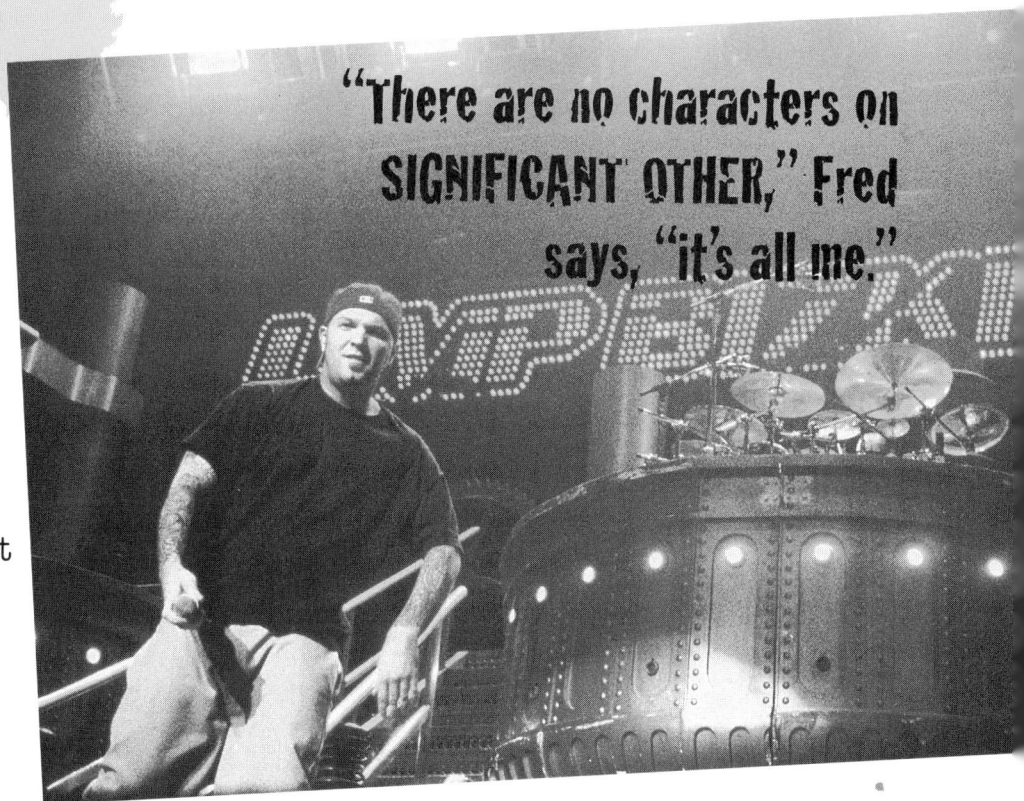

"There are no characters on SIGNIFICANT OTHER," Fred says, "it's all me."

John otto

SAM RIVers

DJ LethAL

Fred Durst

Wes BorLand

THE LIMP BIZKIT STORY

One of the biggest styles in music today is the combo of rap and rock, but it's a tough gig to balance, and no one does it better than Limp Bizkit. Formed in 1994, Limp Bizkit's first single was a cover of George Michael's "Faith." Their popularity has grown steadily since then. Though they've had many career ups and downs nothing has rocked their confidence. Lead singer Fred Durst says, "I've never felt so confident about our focus until right now."

IS ANYBODY OUT THERE?

The music scene of the early '90s in Jacksonville, Florida, was not what Fred Durst was looking for. He was into punk and hip-hop, but the majority of bands in Jacksonville were only doing indie rock or heavy metal. There was no place for Fred to find a niche — so he decided to carve his own.

Fred decided to look for guys that he wanted to play with. He went to every local hot spot to see every band and eventually saw a few guys that he decided to put together. First, he found funk-savvy bassist Sam Rivers, and Sam brought in his cousin John Otto to play drums. When Fred saw Wes Borland play guitar in a punk-metal band he immediately invited him to join the trio and they decided to call themselves Limp Bizkit. The band started playing their style of rock plus hip-hop in the local scene. It was cool because fans loved them, but the guys had no representation, no manager, and no label. "I was acting like I was my own manager on the phone," recalls Fred. "I'd change my voice and I'd change my name and was talking [up] all these record companies." But Fred's clever voices did not get them a record deal. It was not until he met the members of KoRn, in town for a local show, that Limp Bizkit's fortunes began to turn.

He actually met the band in a tattoo parlor — Fred was working there to make ends meet. He worked on the KoRn members and he became particularly friendly with Fieldy. The next time KoRn was in town they hooked up with Fred and he took the opportunity to hand them a demo of his band — KoRn liked the music so much they passed the tape on to their producer, who became an instant believer. The band landed a gig touring with House of Pain and the Deftones (later, when House of Pain split up, DJ Lethal joined Limp Bizkit to round out their sound). The tour was a success and eventually the band signed a contract with a major record label.

FAN APPRECIATION:

Limp Bizkit has always found cool ways to connect with their fans. Touring constantly, Limp Bizkit generated a buzz and even credits the impressive sales of their first album, *Three Dollar Bill Y'all* (released in 1998), to the response of their exciting live performances. The album became a huge hit after the video for "Faith" came out and went into heavy rotation on MTV. Album sales soared to 1.5 million and set the stage for their follow-up album, *Significant Other*, to surpass even that high number — which it did. In its first week in stores Bizkit's second album sold 635,000 copies and knocked the Backstreet Boys' *Millennium* out of the number one spot on the charts.

The boys in Limp Bizkit have not sat back to enjoy their success, however. They have produced an album every year, including the latest one, *Chocolate Starfish and the Hotdog Flavored Water*, which includes eighteen new songs and features such guest artists as KoRn's Jonathan Davis and Kid Rock.

Plus, the band keeps hitting the road for more tours and live shows. They played at Woodstock '99, and then immediately went on to headline The Family Values tour (which they kicked off with three live impromptu shows announced on local radio stations only an hour before they performed in the streets of Boston, Detroit, and Chicago), and they spent the summer of 2000 on their Limpdependence tour, a gig that offered free tickets to fans. Limp Bizkit definitely knows how to appreciate the kids who've made them what they are.

Limp Bizkit has always found cool ways to connect with their fans.

The Kid from Detroit knows how to jam!

CHAPTER 4

KID ROCK

HOW HE CHOSE HIS STAGE NAME: When Kid Rock was young and spinning tables at parties people were so impressed by how good he was they used to say, "Watch that . . . kid rock!"

Name: Robert Ritchie

Birth date: January 17, 1971

Birthplace: Romeo, Michigan

Currently resides in: Royal Oak, Michigan

Musical influences: country, hip-hop, rock, blues, radio, MTV

Musical instruments: vocals, turntables, sampler, guitar, drums

Musical style: a blend of rap-rock, rap-metal, hip-hop, freestyle rap, spaced-out funk, psychedelic rock, jazz, blues, heavy metal samples, and several other genres of music

Family: mother, Susan; father, Bill; brother, Bill Jr.; sisters, Carol and Jill. Kid Rock's son is Robert Ritchie Jr.

Dues paying gigs: pumping gas, car wash attendant, Kmart stock boy

BIGGest Hits:

* "Only God Knows Why"
* "Bawitdaba"
* "Cowboy"

Discography:

* The History of Rock (2000)
* Devil Without a Cause (1998)
* Early Mornin' Stoned Pimp (1996)
* Fire It Up (EP) (1994)
* The Polyfuze Method (1993)
* Grits Sandwiches for Breakfast (1990)

AWARDS/NOMINATIONS:

* 1999 MTV Video Music Award for Best New Artist and Best Rock Video
* 1999 Rolling Stone Male Artist of the Year

THE BAND BEHIND THE MAN:

* Kenny Olson — guitar
* Jason Krause — guitar
* Jimmie Bones — keyboards
* Stefanie Eulinberg — drums
* Matt Shafer — DJ Lethal
* Joe C. — the band's MC

Official website: www.kidrock.com

HOW TO CONTACT:

Kid Rock, c/o Atlantic Records,
9229 Sunset Blvd., Los Angeles, CA, 90069

RANDOM FACTS:

* Kid Rock was born on Super Bowl Sunday
* His hero is country legend Hank Williams because of "his simplicity and his honesty"
* Kid's drummer, Stefanie, sometimes takes the stage in furry animal slippers
* Kid Rock guest starred on a spring break episode of *The Simpsons*
* Kid has his own recording studio named Temple of the Dog

THE KID ROCK STORY

Detroit, Michigan, is well known for being the car manufacturing capital of America. Full of factories and plants, the city is proud of its workforce and its important role in our country's economy. You might not expect there to be a great music scene going on behind the nuts and bolts and soldering that gives the city its reputation, but there *is*, going back as far as Motown (short for "Motor City"). And today, the music scene is still very happening, but instead of rhythm and blues, the hottest sound coming out of Detroit these days is hip-hop. So who's the king of these kinds of tunes? Kid Rock is one of the *most* happening hip-hoppers around. His tunes are on the charts and also have been

featured on MTV's *Beach House*, ESPN's *X-Games*, and even ABC's *Wide World of Sports*.

BORN TO ENTERTAIN

Kid (or Bob Ritchie as his parents named him) grew up in the town of Romeo, a suburb of Detroit. He lived with his parents, two sisters and one brother in a house on 145 acres of apple trees. From as early as the age of six Kid was a performer. Whenever his parents had a party they asked him to entertain, and he never turned down a request. Kid can remember dressing up in his cowboy hat, leather Indian vest, and cowboy boots and running into the party to sing "Bad, Bad, Leroy Brown."

As he grew older, Kid liked the rock 'n' roll tunes coming out of the radio, but he also got into the hip-hop beats. Inspired by the music of Whodini and Run DMC, Kid became a regular on the hip-hop scene. He joined a local breakdancing crew, The Furious Funkers, and started spinning tables when he was in high school. In fact, his mother bought him his first set of turntables for Christmas when he was fourteen. Later, he upgraded his gear with money he earned picking apples in his family's orchard.

By 1987, Kid had moved from his home in Romeo to a pad in nearby Mt. Clemens and became completely immersed in the hip-hop culture. There Kid found a guy on the scene who befriended him and became his tag-team partner. The Blackman, Kid's earliest mentor, helped Kid fit in when they formed a performing duo.

BUSTIN' OUT OF THE SCENE

Kid Rock sharpened his self-taught skills of hyper-speed scratching at basement parties in front of neighborhood crowds and inevitably, he began rapping too. By 1988 he was ready to record his first set of demos, which eventually brought him to the attention of Jive Records. That company signed him to his first record contract. In 1990 Kid's first album, *Grits Sandwiches for Breakfast*, was released. At the same time, Kid landed an opening spot on tour with Ice Cube and Too Short.

While it looked like the Kid was on his way to success, the road was far from smooth. As it turned out, *Grits* didn't sell well at all and Jive dropped him. That's like being fired. At twenty years old, Kid Rock already felt like a hasbeen.

GOING THE INDIE ROUTE

Even though he had been rejected, Kid refused to cave. He kept going, refining and changing his style. He always believed in himself. Looking back over his career, the Kid says, "I knew I could make it work . . . You've got to just be honest with yourself, look in the mirror and say, 'Am I good enough? Do I know I can do something better?' I think that's true with anything you do in life. You've got to be able to compare yourself to other people and say, 'What do I have that's different? Can I compete on that level?' And I always knew I could. There was

Kid Rock & Joe C. share the mic and rock the house while Kenny Olson backs up on guitar.

never even a doubt in my mind." Kid began sampling tunes he really liked and added more rock into his hip-hop.

At the same time, Kid began to build his backup band, Twisted Brown Trucker. The band features two guitarists, a keyboardist, a drummer, and a DJ (who just happens to be Kid's best friend from childhood). The band's sound, southern-fried funk rock, melded perfectly with Kid's disjointed hip-hop style. The last addition to the Kid's entourage was Joe C., a very small man (his growth was stunted from a digestive disorder) who considers himself "the hype man."

Without a record label, however, Kid could not get very far, no matter how tight his act was. When a small independent label expressed an interest in him, Kid signed immediately. The result was the album *The Polyfuze Method* in 1993, and the EP *Fire It Up* in 1994. Unfortunately, the small label was going broke and after the first two albums could not finance another one.

The Kid found himself between a "Rock" and a hard place — he had nowhere to turn. That's when his father stepped up to help out. He helped pay for the new album, which Kid released on his own label, Top Dog Records, in 1996. Since he didn't have a label to distribute the album, Kid sold it on his own, eventually racking up 14,000 sales from his basement apartment.

You could say that Kid owes some of his success to his dad's willingness to give him money: that album became the key to Kid's career takeoff. It got the attention of reps at the major label Atlantic Records who flew to Detroit to catch Kid's show — they were so impressed they signed him immediately.

CLIMBING UP TO THE TOP

In late 1998, Atlantic Records released Kid Rock's debut album, *Devil Without a Cause*, which merges hip-hop with rock. Kid's main collaborator on the album was his best friend, Matt Shaffer (a.k.a. Uncle Kracker). Together they penned most of the songs, including "Only God Knows Why," "Wasting Time," "Cowboy," and "Bawitdaba." The single "Bawitdaba" quickly became one of the hottest songs on radio, while the video for "I Am a Bullgod" got a lot of play on MTV's *Total Request Live*. By July '99, this album, which Kid and his crew wrote and recorded in a little over a week, went double platinum and finally secured Kid a spot at the top of the charts *and* in the center of the hot hip-hop scene.

YOU CAN'T STOP THIS KID

Kid Rock is on a roll. After the success of *Devil Without a Cause* Kid Rock and his band Twisted Brown Trucker went on tour with Limp Bizket, played at Woodstock '99, and did another sell out tour with Metallica in 2000. Kid Rock is branching out into acting, too. His film debut will be in David Spade's film *Joe Dirt* (Kid is doing the title track for the movie too), and he's thinking about starring in a TV sitcom!

Plus, his newest album, *The History of Rock*, was released in May 2000. It features some songs he wrote back in the '80s (for example, "My Oedipus Complex"), as well as several new ones. "I think it's really important for kids to know that I did come from this background that I'm always talking about," he says, "that I have been around for ten years, and I have been writing good songs. I've been writing bad songs [too], but the bottom line is, I've been . . . doing it." With his breakout success and welcome follow-ups it seems Kid Rock will keep on doing it for a long time to come.

HeAd   FIeLdy   Jonathan DAvis   munky   DAvid

CHAPTER 5

KORN

BIGGest Hits:

* * "Somebody Someone"
* * "Make Me Bad"
* * "Freak on a Leash"
* * "Twist"
* * "Good God"
* * "Blind"
* * "Daddy"
* * "Got the Life"

HOW THE BAND GOT ITS NAME: A lot of songwriter Jonathan Davis' inspiration comes from his childhood; the band chose the name of a vegetable and then spelled it in a childlike way, with the "R" sometimes backward, or capitalized.

CITY OF ORIGIN: Bakersfield, California

STYLE OF MUSIC: heavy punk, alternative metal, hardcore rock, rap-metal

OFFICIAL WEBSITE: www.korn.com

FANS CALL THEMSELVES: KoRn Kids

COLLABORATIONS: on *Follow the Leader,* Fred Durst, Travant Hardson, Ice Cube, Cheech Marin

AWARDS/NOMINATIONS:

* 1999 Grammy Award for Best Short Form Music Video for *Freak on a Leash*

* 1999 Best Clip of the Year/Hard Rock; *Billboard* Music Video Award

* 1999 MTV Music Video Award for Best Rock Video for *Freak on a Leash*

RANDOM FACTS:

* KoRn performed two hot songs off the *Issues* album at Woodstock '99
* The cover of *Issues* was designed by one of 20,000 fans who entered a KoRn-sponsored art contest
* Fred Durst (Limp Bizkit) directed KoRn's video "Falling Away From Me"
* KoRn was the first band ever to conduct an interactive radio broadcast on the Internet
* KoRn debuted their song "Falling Away From Me" on the spring break episode of *South Park*

CONTACT THE BAND:

Fans uv KoRn
P.O. Box 931028
Los Angeles, CA 90093

Discography:

* *Issues* (1999)
* *Follow the Leader* (1998)
* *Life Is Peachy* (1996)
* *KoRn* (1994)

THE BOYS IN THE BAND:

Name: Jonathan Davis
Birth date: January 18, 1971
Birthplace: Bakersfield, California
Musical instrument: vocals
Lives now: Belmont Shores, California
Dues paying gigs: manager of a Pizza Hut, janitor

RANDOM FACTS:

* Jonathan began training as a coroner's assistant at the age of sixteen. After seeing so many victims of car crashes he now refuses to drive; he hasn't driven in six years

* Jonathan felt alienated in high school because of his artistic interests
* Jonathan has many tattoos, including the band's logo on his back
* Jonathan has a son named Nathan Houseman Davis

QUOTABLE QUOTES:

* "That's how I deal with life, by screaming about it."
* "We just want to be heavy. All we want to do is bring heavy back into rock 'n' roll."

Name: Reginald Arvizu, aka Fieldy
Birth date: November 2, 1969
Birthplace: Bakersfield, California
Lives now: Belmont Shores, California
Musical instrument: guitar
Dues paying gigs: door-to-door plant salesman

Jonathan Davis

RANDOM FACTS:

* Fieldy is the mastermind behind every piece of KoRn merchandise
* Fieldy is married to his longtime girlfriend, Shela. They have two daughters: Serena and Olivia
* Fieldy has his daughter's name (Serena) tattooed on his neck

QUOTABLE QUOTE:

* To explain how he got his nickname Fieldy says, "When I was younger I had . . . chipmunk cheeks . . . so they called me 'Gopher,' and then it became 'Garf.' Then they started calling me 'Garfield.' Then it [just] became Fieldy."

Name: James Shaffer, aka Munky
Birth date: June 6, 1970
Birthplace: Rosedale, California
Musical instrument: guitar

RANDOM FACTS:

* The tip of one of Munky's fingers was cut off in a biking accident
* The nickname "Munky" comes from the fact that when James' feet are spread out, they look like monkey hands

QUOTABLE QUOTE:

* About his stage persona, Munky says: "It's like that person I don't like in me, all the things I hate about myself, that's who I am up there."

Name: Brian Welch, aka Head
Birth date: June 19, 1970
Birthplace: Torrance, California
Lives now: Redondo Beach, California
Musical instrument: guitar
Dues paying gigs: furniture delivery boy, pizza delivery boy

RANDOM FACTS:

* Before joining the band L.A.P.D. Brian was in a band called Ragtime
* Brian left home at the age of seventeen
* Brian is married to Rebecca; they have a daughter named Jenea Marie Welch
* Brian's nickname "Head" stems from the huge size of his cranium

Name: David Silveria
Birth date: September 21, 1972
Birthplace: Bakersfield, California
Lives now: Huntington Beach, California
Musical instrument: drums
Dues paying gigs: model for skate-punk clothing company 26 Red

RANDOM FACTS:

* David's favorite drummers are Tommy Lee (Mötley Crüe) and Mike Bordin (Faith No More)
* David is married to Shannon Bellino; they have a son named David and a daughter named Sofia Aurora
* David has several tattoos, including Shannon's name, the Cheshire Cat, and the KoRn logo

QUOTABLE QUOTE:

* About his parents' reaction when he said he wanted to be a musician, David says: "My father didn't put me down for this, but he thought I was wasting my time. But my mother was super supportive. She knew it was my dream."

WELCOME TO THE KORN FIELD

Everyone has been picked on in school, but Jonathan Davis, lead singer and songwriter of KoRn, is getting his revenge: Many of his lyrics are about someone who's hurt him. Now he's taking that pain and those experiences and turning them into meaningful songs like "Blind" and "Daddy." That, combined with KoRn's music (a blend of hip-hop, funk, metal, and industrial noise music known as heavy punk) has propelled the band to the top of the charts in both America and around the world.

KORN DOGS

Bakersfield, California, is not exactly a place Jonathan likes to revisit. There are bad memories there about his parents' divorce and his bad relationship with his father's new wife. Plus, the dusty working-class mining town north of Los Angeles had little to offer in terms of entertainment. Although Jonathan may have hated it, most of the inspiration for his songs now comes from how miserable he was back then. Today, he's turning those angry and sad emotions into great music, helping KoRn to become one of the most influential alternative rock bands on the scene.

While Bakersfield may not be Jonathan's favorite place, it does hold the great honor of being where he met bassist Reg "Fieldy" Arvizu, drummer David Silveria, and guitarists James "Munky" Shaffer and Brian "Head" Welch. In fact, the Bakersfield area is where all the guys grew up, and it is where they first formed their heavy metal punk band. Sometimes dubbed "the Backstreet Boys of metal," KoRn has two best-selling albums (*Life Is Peachy* and *Issues*), their own record label (Elementree), a cool website, and a weekly Internet after-school special called KoRn TV. Plus they're kings of mega-concerts — from headlining Lollapalooza to Woodstock '99. They are even the masterminds behind the popular summer concert tour, Family Values.

KORN KERNELS

While their success may be recent, the truth is, these guys have known each other since before high school. Fieldy used to pick on Jonathan when they were kids — he even ran Jonathan over with a three-wheeler. They knew each other because their dads used to play in a band together. Now Fieldy is following in his father's footsteps by playing guitar.

But Jonathan and Fieldy are not the only band members who've known each other a long time. Some of the other guys have been playing music together since they were teenagers. Munky and Brian became friends in high school and played in the band L.A.P.D. together. They even eventually added David and Fieldy to the band. Speaking of whom, David and Fieldy had hooked up when David was just thirteen and he inquired about a vacant drummer's position in Fieldy's band. After a single tryout David got the gig and has been making music ever since. "My father offered to pay my whole way to college," David says, "but I told him I wanted to try this first."

When Fieldy, Munky, David, and Head all got together in L.A.P.D. the band changed its name to Creep before finally settling on KoRn. But they were still missing a lead

HEAd

singer. One night they were out catching some local bands at a club in Bakersfield. As they were leaving they heard Jonathan start to sing. They stayed for his whole set — and then immediately approached him to join their band. The year was 1993.

REINVENTING PUNK

Because KoRn pretty much invented the blend of modern-rock rage and funky hip-hop, you could call them one of the biggest musical pioneers of the 1990s. "We're not out to change the world," Jonathan says on behalf of the band, "just music." You could certainly say they've accomplished that goal considering their very first album was the first debut hardcore rock act to top the charts. It even went platinum. That was in 1994 and it came after the band had played over 200 shows.

The album was called simply *KoRn* and was a sort of story about childhood. "Blind" was the first single and it upped KoRn's fan base when the video got a lot of play on late-night MTV shows.

Like many other punk bands, KoRn has gotten and maintained a lot of their success through their live performances. In 1996 KoRn released their follow-up album, *Life Is Peachy.* Again they soared to the top of the charts, this time with songs like "Twist" and "Good God."

The ride to the top has not stopped. The year 1998 saw the release of the band's third album, *Follow the Leader,* their biggest hit to date. The singles "Got the Life" and "Freak on a Leash" became hugely popular and solidified the band's high profile punk status. While all of KoRn's music is intensely personal and based on the band's private experiences, their fourth album is the one most deeply emotional.

Issues, released in 1999, is "a concept thing," explains Jonathan, "about how I went through [a bad time personally] when *Follow the Leader* came out and we did [the] Family Values tour . . . The whole thing's based on . . . one long story." Mostly, it is the story of Jonathan's feelings about the pressures of fame, success, and the breakup of his marriage. The lyrics recount, he explains, "a big transformation in my life, and it's me just writing it all out . . . It's almost a solo album it's so personal." As it turns out, Jonathan's feelings, as reflected in his music, touched a nerve with KoRn's fans. Since its 1999 release *Issues* has sold over three million copies in the United States alone. The guys hit the road for a big summer 2000 tour with Metallica. KoRn may have begun as an "underground" thrash-rock band, but they're in the forefront of the music scene now. At the rate they're going, it looks like they'll stay on the top of the punk movement for a long time to come.

Korn pauses for a photo after accepting their MTV Music Video Award.

The Legendary Carlos Santana

CHAPTER 6

SANTANA/ matchbox twenty's Rob Thomas

Name: Carlos Santana
Birth date: July 20, 1947
Birthplace: Autlant de Navarro, Mexico
Lives now: San Rafael, California
Instruments: guitar, violin
Musical influences: BB King, John Lee Hooker, T. Bone Walker
Musical style: Latin rock + blues + Afro-Cuban rhythms
Official website: www.santana.com

HOW TO CONTACT:

* Carlos Santana, c/o Creative Artists Agency, 9830 Wilshire Blvd., Beverly Hills, Califorina 90212

* Fanclub@santana.com

CARLOS SANTANA's BIGGest hits:

* "Smooth"
* "Maria Maria"
* "Evil Ways"
* "Black Magic Woman"

Dues paying gigs:
* Selling Chiclets and spearmint on the street in Tijuana
* Shining shoes
* Playing Mexican folk songs on the street for fifty cents
* Street musician in San Francisco
* Waiter/busboy in San Francisco

Family: wife, Deborah; son, Salvador; daughters, Stella and Anjelica

AWARDS/NOMINATIONS:

✳ Carlos Santana was nominated for eleven Grammys at the 42nd Grammy Awards on February 23, 2000. He won nine of them, tying him with Michael Jackson as the only artist to win so many Grammys in one night. The awards were for:

1. **Record of the Year:** "Smooth"
2. **Album of the Year:** *Supernatural*
3. **Song of the Year**: "Smooth"
4. **Best Pop Collaboration with vocals:** "Smooth" with Rob Thomas
5. **Best Pop Instrumental:** "El Farol"
6. **Best Rock Performance by a Duo or Group:** "Put Your Lights On" with Everlast
7. **Best Rock Instrumental:** "The Calling" with Eric Clapton
8. **Best Rock Album:** *Supernatural*
9. **Best Rock Performance by a Duo or Group with vocals:** "Maria Maria"

✳ At the 30th Grammy Award show in 1988 Carlos received a Grammy Award for Best Rock Instrumental

✳ Carlos was inducted into the Rock and Roll Hall of Fame in 1998

✳ Carlos was inducted into the Hollywood Rock Walk in 1996

✳ In 1996 *Billboard* magazine awarded Carlos the Century Award, their highest honor for lifetime creative achievement

✳ Carlos was given a star on the Hollywood Walk of Fame in 1998

THE BAND BEHIND THE MAN:

✳ Chester Thompson — keyboards
✳ Benny Rietveld — bass guitar
✳ Rodney Holmes — drums
✳ Raul Rekow — congas, percussion

* Karl Perazzo — timbales, percussion
* Tony Lindsay — vocals
* Andy Vargas — vocals

RANDOM FACTS:

* Carlos' early combo, The Santana Band, was the first to earn CBS Record's Crystal Globe Award for sales of more than five million internationally.
* Carlos believes he is visited by the ghosts of Miles Davis, Zapáta (a revolutionary Mexican hero), Geronimo, Che Guevara, and Pancho Villa

QUOTABLE QUOTE:

* When the president of Arista Records called to tell Carlos that *Supernatural* had gone seven times platinum, Santana said: "I'm glad I'm lying down or else I'd fall."

Carlos & Rob Thomas make some "Smooth" music together.

matchbox twenty's Rob Thomas

Name: Robert Kelly Thomas

Birth date: February 14, 1972

Birthplace: American military base in Germany

Raised in: Florida and South Carolina

Family: wife, Marisol

Favorite music: Ani Di Franco, Elvis Costello, James Brown, Al Greene, Elton John

Musical instruments: lead vocals, piano, guitar

Musical influences: Van Morrison, Elton John, Elvis Costello, Bernie Taupin, Tom Petty, Al Greene

Dues paying gigs: Rob used to play piano at parties in exchange for a place to sleep

Musical style: post-grunge guitar-pop

Official website: www.matchboxtwenty.com

HOW TO CONTACT:

matchbox twenty, c/o Atlantic Records, 1290 Avenue of the Americas, New York, New York 10104

AWARDS/NOMINATIONS:

Three Grammy Awards for "Smooth" off Santana's *Supernatural* album (2000): Best Pop Collaboration, Song of the Year, Record of the Year; Grammy nomination for matchbox twenty's hit single "Push" (1998); Grammy nomination for Best Rock Performance by a Duo or Group (1998); BMI Award, Pop Songwriter of the Year (1999)

MATCHBOX twenty's BIGGest hits:

* "Bent"
* "Push"
* "3 a.m."

DiscoGraphy:

* mad season by matchbox twenty (2000)
* Yourself or Someone Like You (1996)

THE BAND BEHIND THE MAN:

* Kyle Cook — guitar
* Adam Gaynor — guitar
* Brian Yale — bass
* Paul Doucette — drums

RANDOM FACTS:

* The name "matchbox twenty" came about when Rob saw a matchbox with a cool logo and then noticed someone wearing a jersey with the number twenty on it
* "matchbox twenty" is always written in lower case
* The band's first album, *Yourself or Someone Like You*, has gone platinum ten times— it sold over ten million copies

ROB ThOMAs

* Rob has a chipped front tooth — a casualty from an evening of slam dancing in Daytona Beach, Florida
* Rob's hidden talent is cooking

QUOTABLE QUOTE:

* "Everything I'm writing about is very personal to me. But if you hang with [the band] for a couple of days, you'd see that we're such goofballs, it's pitiful."

THE SANTANA STORY

The beginning of the year 2000 saw an unprecedented explosion in the popularity of Latino music. Stars like Ricky Martin, Jennifer Lopez, Mark Anthony, The Buena Vista Social Club, and Enrique Iglesias have brought the African-based rhythms of the Latin culture to the forefront of the music scene. But these young performers are not the first to hit the charts with the beat of their culture's music. In the 1960s Carlos Santana and his band achieved international success with their rhythmic blend of rock, blues, and Afro-Cuban influence. After a legendary performance at the original Woodstock concert in 1969, Santana hit it big and won fans with such songs as "Evil Ways" and "Black Magic Woman."

Over the next thirty years Santana released thirty-five albums, including eight that went platinum and eight that went gold. But no one stays on top all the time. During the '80s and most of the '90s, sales for Santana's music slumped. And then came *Supernatural.* The year was 1999, and Santana surprised everyone, including himself, when his new album shot to the top of the charts. It contained the number one song at the dawn of the twenty-first century, "Smooth," and to date has sold over ten million copies worldwide.

FROM MEXICO TO SAN FRANCISCO

One of seven children, Carlos Santana was born in 1947 in a small town in Mexico. His father was a mariachi violinist and taught him to play the violin at the age of five. When the family moved to Tijuana in 1955 Carlos began to study the guitar. He realized that while he enjoyed the traditional forms of music his father introduced him to, he much preferred the pumping tunes of rock 'n' roll. As a teenager Carlos began performing with local bands in Tijuana until his family moved again, in 1961. This time, the Santana clan ended up in San Francisco, California — in the USA. It was here that Carlos began to create his own personal style of music.

THE RISE AND FALL OF SANTANA

By 1966 Carlos had developed a distinct sound that blended many genres. Feeling that his music was ready for the public, Carlos formed his own band, The Santana Blues Band, which played a unique fusion of Afro-Latin and rock. "We were told we were crazy playing the music we played," remembers Gregg Rolie, one of Carlos' initial vocalists. "But it was original. To this day, nothing sounds like it." The sound was so unique, in fact, that the band was invited to play at Woodstock in 1969, an event that led to them signing their first record deal with Columbia Records. In those days, it was run by Clive Davis, who has remained a great supporter throughout Carlos' long career.

Everyone's career has ups and downs, and by 1997 Carlos wanted to do something that would skyrocket his music again. At the suggestion of Deborah, his wife, Carlos called his old friend Clive Davis and together they worked out a strategy to put Carlos back on the charts. To Clive, the most important thing to do was to get Carlos back on the airwaves, and the quickest way to do that was to reach a younger audience. The quickest way to do *that* was to pair Carlos with several young, hot artists. That's exactly what they did — and Clive's plan worked brilliantly.

SUPERNATURAL SUCCESS

The musical celebrities Carlos chose to work with on the record were as varied as Carlos' own musical style. He explains that "every musician who participated [in the making of the album] was on the same wavelength and artistic energy as I was . . . *Supernatural* is a beautiful example of synchronicity." The list of guest stars includes Rob Thomas, Wyclef Jean, Lauryn Hill, Eric Clapton, Everlast, Dave Matthews, Eagle Eye Cherry, and Mana.

Most of the musicians came to the project with their own songs. The only true writing collaboration was between Carlos and Dave Matthews. They went into the studio and together wrote and recorded "Love of My Life." Says Dave of how it worked, "[Carlos] gave me some lyrics, a couple of lines, and I didn't know what to do. I think he wrote it about his father." Carlos agrees, the song is about his father, who died a few years ago.

Other collaborations worked a little differently. For example, Eric Clapton didn't have any material, so he and Carlos went into the studio and jammed and then Carlos made a song out of it. While many of the songs on *Supernatural* have become successful radio tunes, there is one song that blasted off the charts, "Smooth," Carlos' collaboration with Rob Thomas, frontman of matchbox twenty.

SANTANA + MATCHBOX TWENTY = AWARD-WINNING COMBUSTION

In 1996 an album was released that combined the sounds of '70s arena rock with '90s American alternarock. The album was called *Yourself or Someone Like You,* and the band was matchbox twenty, five guys who had gotten together in Orlando, Florida. While critics didn't go wild about the album, fans dug the band's blend of Pearl Jam and REM sound.

While Rob Thomas is the lead singer of the band, there are four other members, including Rob's good friends Paul Doucette and Brian Yale. Together Rob, Paul, and Brian drifted through various bands in Orlando before forming matchbox 20 by adding Adam Gaynor and Kyle Cook. In 1995 a record producer heard the band and helped them make some demos (demonstration tapes) that eventually landed them a recording contract. matchbox twenty's first single, "Long Day," managed to get enough radio play to pave the way for their next single, "Push," to climb the charts. That began a string of hits that kept the band's debut album on the charts for almost two years.

To support the album, the band went on a long and extensive international tour throughout Canada, Australia, and New Zealand. Exhausted from touring, matchbox twenty set aside 1999 as the year to record their second album, *mad season by matchbox twenty.* When asked about their approach to creating the new tunes, Rob says, "When we made our first record, we hadn't really been a band for very long. We hadn't had any really good fights, we hadn't had any really good laughs, we hadn't done much of anything together. But [by 1999] so much has happened to us that we've formed a character within ourselves. So this is really the first time we're saying, 'This is matchbox twenty making a record,' because now matchbox twenty is its own entity. This is the first one where we can really say, *this is our sound.*"

The band was stoked to stop touring and begin creating again. *mad season by matchbox twenty* marks a change in both the band's style and the development of their music. It is the first time other members of the band have contributed songs. Usually Rob writes everything and the band plays what he gives them. Paul Doucette explains, "Rob brings us songs that he has. He writes them on the acoustic guitar or the piano, and then he plays them for us. Then we just sort of take it from there and add everything else to it." On the new album, however, Paul and Kyle also share composing credits.

ROB THOMAS + SANTANA = GRAMMY TIME

Born on an American military base in Germany, Rob Thomas spent his childhood shuttling between his mother's home in Florida and his grandmother's home in South Carolina. When he was old enough to be on his own, he settled in Orlando, Florida. It was there that he learned to play piano when a friend agreed to teach him. Together, Rob and his friend formed a band that played in Florida-area hotels. It wasn't until 1995, when Rob joined a band called Tabitha's Secret, that Rob met Paul and Brian, and his musical career began to take off.

The success of *Yourself or Someone Like You* brought Rob and his band fame and fortune. It also brought him to the attention of Carlos' producer, who sent the backing track for "Smooth" to Rob. Initially, they were only interested in Rob adding some different lyrics and melody; they were thinking of asking George Michael to sing the song. But when Carlos heard the tape that Rob sent back, singing to demonstrate the changes he had made, Carlos insisted on having Rob record the song himself. The resulting Latin-flavored, mid-tempo rock song "Smooth" was an instant success. According to Carlos, "Some songs are just like tattoos for your brain . . . you hear them and they're affixed to you." You can say that again — and again!

MAtchBOx twɘnfy

Brian YALɘ

KYLɘ COOK

ROB ThOMAs

PAuL Doucɘttɘ

Adam GAYLC

CHAPTER 7

DAVE MATTHEWS BAND

Name: Dave Matthews

Birth date: January 9, 1967

Birthplace: Johannesburg, South Africa

Lives now: Blue Ridge Mountains in Virginia

Musical instrument: lead vocals, guitar

Musical influences: INXS, Traffic, Peter Gabriel, U2

Musical style: jazz + fusion + funk + rock

Dues paying gigs: bartender, research clerk at IBM

Official website: www.davematthewsband.com

BIGGest HitS:
* "Satellite"
* "Crash into Me"
* "Crush"
* "So Much to Say"
* "Tripping Billies"

HOW TO CONTACT: fanmail@dmband.com

AWARDS/NOMINATIONS:

* Grammy Award, "So Much to Say"; Best Rock Performance by a duo or group (1997)
* Grammy Nominations, "Crash into Me"; Best Rock Performance by a duo or group with Vocal, Best Rock Song (1997)
* MTV Video Award Nomination, *Crash into Me;* Best Group Video and Best Rock Video (1997)

THE BAND BEHIND THE MAN:

* Leroi Moore — saxophone
* Carter Beauford — drums
* Stefan Lessard — bass
* Boyd Tinsley — violin

RANDOM FACTS:

* DMB headlined Woodstock '99
* Dave is the youngest member in his family
* The first official gig DMB played was on May 11, 1991, at a private rooftop party in Charlottesville, Virginia

QUOTABLE QUOTE:

* Dave is very modest about his contribution to the band, even though it bears his name. According to him, he's the least competent musician on the stage! And if you ask who's the leader of the band, he'll tell you: "The way I look at it, we have five lead voices in this band. I may be the first thing people notice, since I do all the singing, but there are times when Leroi's sax is the voice, and times when Boyd is at the front . . . There are very few times when the audience has just one thing to listen to."

LOOK FOR: The Dave Matthews Band will perform in the upcoming IMAX rock concert movie, *All Access.* Also on the bill, Kid Rock, Santana, and Rob Thomas.

Discography:

* Live at Luther College (1999)
* Listener Supported (1999)
* Before These Crowded Streets (1998)
* Crash (1996)
* Live at Red Rocks (1995)
* Under the Table and Dreaming (1994)
* Remember Two Things (1993)

Dave

THE DAVE MATTHEWS BAND STORY

The Dave Matthews Band got started in Charlottesville, Virginia, where their very first gigs were played at the University of Virginia. That was back in the early '90s. Soon, word of the band's hip sound of pop mixed with jazz-fusion had spread all the way across the country to Colorado. Ten years later, that word of mouth turned the Dave Matthews Band into a huge international success.

OUT OF SOUTH AFRICA

At the tender age of two, Dave Matthews moved with his family from a suburb of Johannesburg, South Africa, to Yorktown Heights, just north of New York City. Dave's dad was a physicist and got transferred to the United States to do research. Dave's mother was an architect. The Matthews clan was one big happy family. Dave grew up with two sisters and a brother — all of them were extremely close. Tragically, when Dave was ten, his father died of lung cancer. Three years later his mom decided to move the family back to South Africa. By that time, young Dave was already a huge music fan and could play the acoustic guitar. Even today, all these years and successful albums later, it's the instrument closest to his heart. "I feel at home with an acoustic [guitar]," he says, "because it's hollow; it's got a drum quality." That skins sound is what Dave likes best. In South Africa one of his earliest influences was African music, which relies heavily on drums. Now, when he composes, rhythm plays a big role in the beginning of any song. "I'm very into percussion," Dave explains. "That's the way songwriting started for me: imitating different folk music that I found, drumming in African…music." When he was a teenager Dave became serious about music as a possible career choice, and even formed his own metal band.

Dave didn't stay in South Africa much past his teen years. Instead he returned to New York where he found a job as a temporary employee at IBM. But soon he decided to live in Charlottesville, Virginia, because his dad had taught school there before Dave was born. By 1987 Dave was settled in the southern town and had a job as a bartender at a local hangout. Just when things seemed to settling down for him, tragedy struck again. His sister and her husband were killed in South Africa. Dave was devastated, but today he says that the pain he has felt in his life he uses in his songs. "I think a lot of the reason my choruses conclude 'Make the best of it' — or maybe, 'Be grateful, anyway' — is because the different tragedies that hit our family were also an *inspiration* for me. They make me want to live now . . . and try to affect things positively."

MAKING THE BAND

If Dave was so passionate about his music, why didn't he pursue it as soon as he returned to the U.S.? Well, back in those days, Dave was very shy about his music and writing. He didn't tell any of his American friends about it until 1990. That's when he decided to record some demo tapes and wanted a band behind him. As Leroi, his saxophone player, recalls, "[Dave and I] used to get into these weird conversations. . . . [But they weren't about music.] I had no idea Dave was a musician. Not the slightest idea. He was just the bartender."

But when Dave *was* ready to record, he turned to the people he had become friends with and drafted them into his band.

First, Dave approached a saxophone player he knew, Leroi Moore. Leroi had begun playing sax in the band at school in seventh grade and by 1990 was one of the most respected and sought-after players in Charlottesville. Next Dave invited Carter Beauford to play drums. It just so happens, Carter and Leroi had grown up together and were good friends. After college they even played in a band together, so Carter joined in. At the time, Carter was playing in several bands doing different types of music, everything from swing to jazz. He says he agreed to play for Dave because "the tape Dave gave me grabbed me immediately. It wasn't jazz, it wasn't rock, it wasn't folk — it was something totally different."

The next player Dave needed was a bass and for that, he asked a friend who recommended sixteen-year-old musical prodigy Stefan Lessard. Stefan signed on immediately. The band found its last member in violinist Boyd Tinsley, another local musician.

The newly formed Dave Matthews Band spent the next two years playing 200 shows a year(!!), developing their unique sound. Mostly they played at college fraternity parties and in local clubs. Lucky for them, the owner of one of the clubs caught the act and decided to manage them.

GRASS ROOTS GROWTH

The band's new manager, Coran, "fit right into the Dave Matthews state of mind." Early on the band agreed to encourage their fans to make tape recordings of their performances. Fans loved this idea and the tapes were copied and distributed all over the university campus and eventually even across the country. By word of mouth and those free tapes, the Dave Matthews Band sound spread around. And Coran decided to make the most of it.

As the band's fan base grew, many record companies developed an interest in signing them, but Coran and the group turned them down, deciding instead to "grow their name" until they felt they were big enough for a major label deal.

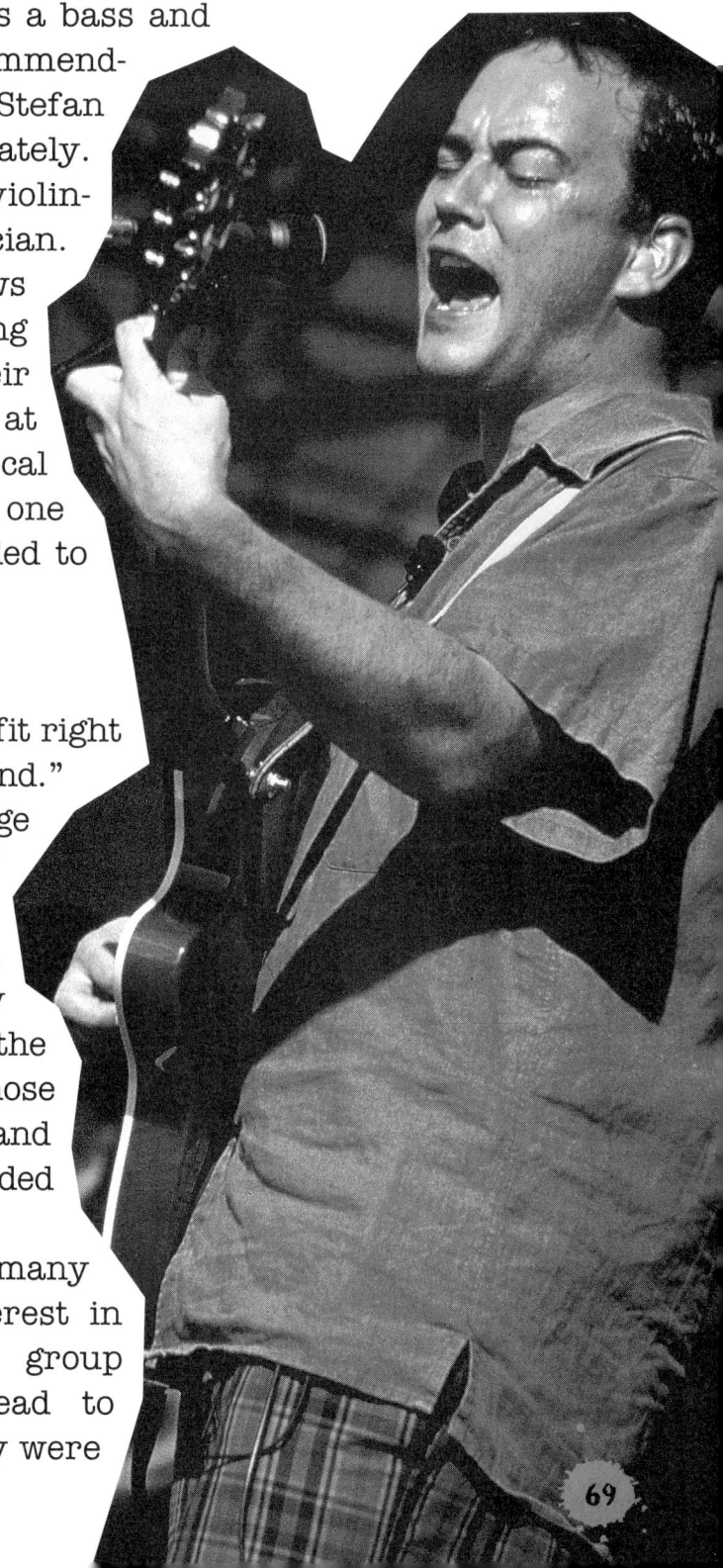

In 1993, then, the band released, their first album by themselves on their very own label, Bama Rags. The album was called *Remember Two Things.* It debuted on college music charts as the highest independent entry ever. DMB kept touring, their collection of fans kept growing, and by the end of 1993 they finally agreed to sign a recording contract with RCA Records.

SWIMMNG IN THE MAINSTREAM

The first record released on the new label was *Under the Table and Dreaming;* it was an instant success. Again, the band hit the road and wrote the music for their next album while they were on tour. In the meantime, they released a concert album called *Live at Red Rocks.* The album was another big success and proved that DMB had definitely made the leap from a grass-roots local band to hot musical superstars.

In 1996 they went back into the studio and recorded *Crash.* The song "Crash into Me" became a *huge* hit and increased DMB's fame. Now the band started an even bigger tour, in bigger sold out venues. Instead of

being the supporting act, they were the headliners. Were the guys overwhelmed by their success? Nope. Because it all happened so gradually, they're comfortable with the stardom. "It's been pretty natural because it hasn't happened that fast. We didn't change within the band and we didn't rush it." Carter agrees. "We never once tried to make this thing become what it is," he says. "It just happened." And the guys just went with the flow.

In 1998 DMB went back into the studio and released their third RCA album, *Before These Crowded Streets.* DMB has been known for their happy and optimistic sound and lyrics, but this album showed another side of Dave. *Before* was more introspective. "I've always been frustrated about all sorts of things," Dave says, "but music was a way I could get past it. In most instances, music and anger don't meet up for me; but on [*Before*] they do. It's sort of a release." Another new twist to the album was the number of guest stars who appeared on it, including rock superstar Alanis Morissette.

Back on tour again, the band put out two live albums in 1999: *Listener Supported* and *Live at Luther College* (this album shows off Dave's acoustic abilities, proving that despite his fame he hasn't forgotten his musical roots). Also in 1999 the band appeared on the hugely successful Santana comeback album, *Supernatural*, with the song "Love of My Life."

What's up next for this mega-hit band? They went back into the studio in 2000 to record their fourth label album, but this time they're doing things a little differently. Instead of writing all the songs on the road, they are writing them in the studio. Usually DMB tests out new songs at their live performances, but for this album Dave wants to challenge himself more as a songwriter and so he's taking some time and much needed privacy. "Sometimes I get a little afraid that being on the road . . . I will lose sight of some of the things that were inspirational to me when I was bartending and meeting people." Dave doesn't need to worry that he's losing his touch. No matter what Dave does, he always comes out on top.

The "All Stars" in Smash Mouth are Steve, Paul, Greg

CHAPTER 8

SMASH MOUTH

CURRENT BAND RESIDENCE: San Jose, California
STYLE OF MUSIC: ska-punk/popcore
OFFICIAL WEBSITE: www.smashmouth. com

HOW TO CONTACT: Smash Mouth, c/o Interscope Records, 2220 Colorado, Avenue, Santa Monica, California 90404

AWARDS/NOMINATIONS:

✳ Grammy nomination for Best Pop Performance by a Duo or Group with Vocal; "All Star" (2000)

RANDOM FACT:

✳ The title of Smash Mouth's debut album, *Fush Yu Mang,* is taken from an Al Pacino line in *Scarface*

Name: Steven Scott Harwell
Birth date: January 9, 1967
Birthplace: Santa Clara, California
Instrument: vocals — he's the lead singer
Musical influences: Elvis, reggae, rap

BIGGest Hits:
✳ "When the Morning Comes"
✳ "All Star"
✳ "Walkin' on the Sun"

RANDOM FACT:

✳ Steve Harwell's main musical idol is Elvis Presley (he has an Elvis tattoo on his forearm and an Elvis telephone that sings "Jailhouse Rock" when it rings). When he was growing up, Steve sang famous Elvis songs for his family — whether they liked it or not!

QUOTABLE QUOTE:

✳ "Someone once told me that you meet the same people on the way up that you do on the way down, so I've been trying to look at at things that way and avoid burning bridges."

Name: Gregory Dean Camp
Birth date: April 2, 1967
Birthplace: West Covina, California
Instrument: guitar, vocals, songwriter
Musical influences: The Carpenters, Johnny Cash, José Feliciano, Kiss, Van Halen

QUOTABLE QUOTE:

* "We formed a band with the intention of getting on the radio and making a record. It wasn't about trying to be cool."

Name: Paul De Lisle
Birth date: June 13, 1963
Birthplace: Exeter, Ontario, Canada
Instrument: bass, vocals
Musical influences: Van Halen, Kiss, Aerosmith, Foghat

Discography:
* *East Bay Season* (1999)
* *Astro Lounge* (1999)
* *Fush Yu Mang* (1997)

QUOTABLE QUOTE:

* What Paul likes about his best bandmate Greg: "He's a skateboarder and a surfer; he understands [the surf] culture and he's a brilliant musician. When we met, I said, 'Dude, I've been looking for you my whole life.'"

Name: Mitch Marine
Birth date: October 8, 1961
Birthplace: Morton, Illinois
Instrument: drums

RANDOM FACTS:

* Mitch began playing drums in eighth grade
* Mitch is a golf nut
* Mitch is married to Jenny Jopling
* Mitch attended North Texas University

BAND BACKUPS:
* Mike Klooster — keyboards
* Mark Cervantes — percussion

THE SMASH MOUTH STORY

Most bands have a distinct style that defines them every time one of their songs is heard on the radio. Not Smash Mouth. This hip foursome, who hail from San Jose, California, don't want to be musically typecast. The ultimate party band, Smash Mouth's musical style has a little of everything, including surf and garage influences along with Latin funk, ska, popcore, soul, surf-punk, and laid-back punk, not to mention ska-thrash with a little hip-hop thrown into their background. Says guitarist Greg Camp, "Put every style in a blender on high . . . mix it together, pour yourself a cup . . . and that's us. I don't want this band to be considered a punk band, a ska band, a surf band, a rock band, a pop band. I just want to be considered Smash Mouth; however people interpret it, it is what it is." Not many bands would be brave enough to comfortably glide from one style to another, but the four guys in Smash Mouth thrive and survive on not being confined by any kind of boundaries.

GROWING UP TO BE SMASHING

The members of Smash Mouth have grown up with each other. Drummer Kevin Coleman and singer Steve Harwell have known each other since grade school. In fact, they formed their own garage band when they were thirteen. Since they were not old enough to drive, Steve used to put his Fender amplifier in a shopping cart and wheel it over to Kevin's house every day, one mile each way.

Steve HArwELL →

75

After their freshman year of high school Kevin transferred to another school and the guys played in different bands. Inspired by such acts as House of Pain, Steve joined a local hip-hop group, F.O.S., and even had a short-lived deal with a record label. When it fell apart, Steve and Kevin hooked up again. In 1994 Steve's manager introduced them to guitarist Greg Camp who was playing with a local cover band called Lackadaddy. Greg remembers, "[Steve and Kevin] came to my house just about every morning at ten, banging on my window. They really wanted me to be in this project. They brought songs with just drums and lyrics, so I helped them write." Soon, Greg brought in bassist Paul De Lisle and the guys named themselves Smash Mouth, a term taken from NFL coach Mike Ditka, who had labeled a particularly rough game as "smash mouth football."

PAUL DeLISLE

The new foursome immediately began writing and rehearsing. Right away they knew they were good together. "The first time we played," remembers Greg, "I knew we had it." The guys found common ground in their shared interest in surf music, ska, and '60s pop. They recorded several songs together in the bedroom of Greg's apartment. Says Steve of the band's initial motivation, "When we formed the band, we didn't have one style of music in mind. We just decided we were going to write songs that feel good to us." And they became all stars doing just that.

THE CARSON CONNECTION

One night Kevin borrowed a practice eight-track tape that contained some of Greg's old songs, including an early version of "Walkin' on the Sun." When Kevin got home and heard the song he went back and woke up Greg at two in the morning to tell him, "Dude, we have to do this song!"

Smash Mouth made more demo tapes and played on the local band scene in San Jose, San Francisco, and Los Angeles. Finally, they caught the ear of a producer who helped them make a two-song demo. It was so good that Steve and Greg decided the music had to hit the airwaves, with or without a record deal.

Anxious to get their music on the radio, Steve and Greg went down to San Jose station KOME and convinced KOME DJ at the time — Carson Daly!! — to listen to their tape. Carson flipped over a tune called "Nervous in the Alley," and "Before we knew it, we were the only unsigned band in regular rotation on KOME," recalls Steve. In fact, the song became so popular the station had to pull it from rotation because fans were calling to ask where the song could be purchased — and it couldn't!

Now the band's success took on a life of its own and the band's popularity grew until KOME invited Smash Mouth to play at the station's Kamp KOME festival on the bill with other bands such as No Doubt, Beck, and 311. The result of Smash Mouth's local appearance was a lot of press coverage and sudden record label interest, but they still had no deal. Undaunted, the band spent their own money to go into the recording studio in 1997 planning to record an album and release it themselves if they could not find label support. Luckily, Interscope Records was interested in the band and signed them immediately.

FUSH YU MANG

Smash Mouth's debut album, *Fush Yu Mang*, in 1997, took only a month to record. The majority of songs were played live. The only additional instruments are horns and keyboards on a few songs. Although

"Walkin' on the Sun" was the breakout song of this album, it is not an accurate sample of what the other tracks sound like — they're more melodic/pop oriented. Steve and Greg worried about what fan reactions would be, but according to Steve, "It did kind of freak people out . . . because ["Walkin' on the Sun"] is so different from the rest of the album, but most of the people we've talked to have told us they enjoy the album because you can listen to it from front to back, and every song has its own style."

Most of the songs, both music and lyrics, are written by Greg, but the band maintains that it is the creative combination of the team that turns the music into what fans hear. "All the songs are written on an acoustic guitar," Greg explains. "Then I take the bare skeletons to the band so they can add their parts and personalities." The final product contained thirteen tracks. Mixed in to the band's ska-based sound are some '50s science-fiction sound effects, Beach Boys-like background vocals, and even some Cuban folk rhythms. While "Walkin' on the Sun" became a number one modern rock hit, the album itself went on to sell more than two million copies.

NO ONE-HIT WONDER

A lot of bands have one hit song and then never hit the charts again. Usually this happens because their one breakout song doesn't sound like any of their other music — and fans want to hear more of what they liked. The challenge for Smash Mouth, then, was to make sure that their follow-up album was as good as the first one and didn't tank on the charts.

Supported by a large recording budget this time around, Smash Mouth returned to the studio in August 1998 and recorded *Astro Lounge*, a fifteen-track album with lots of different sounds. In order to generate excitement for the record, the band leaked the first new single, "All Star," before the album was released. It's an incredibly inspirational song about how you can be whatever you want to be, and no matter what you do, you are a star. The single hit the charts almost at the top and propelled the album to fabulous sales. *Astro Lounge* was such a success that Smash

Mouth was nominated for a Grammy Award in the category of Best Pop Performance by a Duo or Group with Vocal.

Unfortunately, while things were going well for the band, things were not going so well for Kevin Coleman. A few years ago he was in a car accident and hurt his back. The harsh touring schedule of the band turned out to be bad for the injuries he had received and so he quit Smash Mouth at the end of 1999. For now, Mitch Marine is filling in for Kevin while the band continues to tour. And they're introducing him as their "new drummer," even though there's no word yet on who Kevin's permanent replacement will be. Mitch, though, is a seasoned pro. He has played in several different bands over the years and often works as a studio musician. Of his gig with Smash Mouth Mitch says he's psyched to get "a chance to lay down a real solid rock beat for a great band and a great songwriter."

SIMPLY SMASHING

So how does Smash Mouth feel about their success? "It doesn't really hit until we're sitting around . . ." says Steve, "and we'll all start laughing at each other and say, 'We sold a million records!'" It seems the band is in the center of the current music scene and has found a formula that will allow them to stay. While Smash Mouth is the ultimate party band, don't ever sell them short; these hip

GrEG GAMp

wiseguys of ska punk also have a soft side and try, through their music, to get a message across to their fans. Every one of their songs has a significant meaning and shows their philosophies, especially their belief that "good will and racial harmony can be spread through good tunes" — not a bad motto for four surfers from San Jose. Or for anyone!

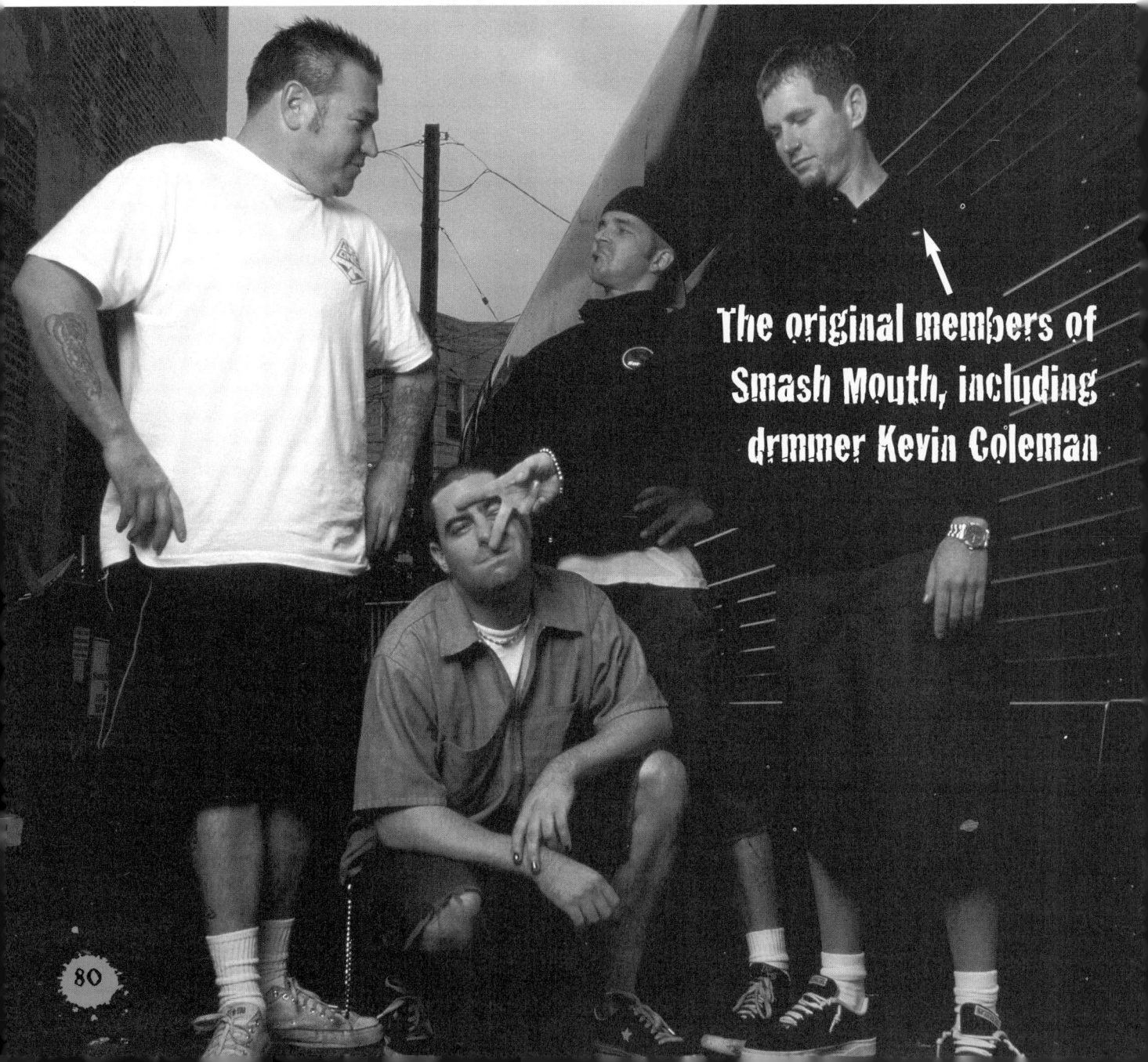

The original members of Smash Mouth, including drmmer Kevin Coleman

CHAPTER 9
RED HOT CHILI PEPPERS

BIGGest Hits:

* "Under the Bridge"
* "Give It Away"
* "Scar Tissue"
* "Love Rollercoaster"
* "Other Side"

HOW THE BAND GOT THEIR NAME:
According to band member Flea, Red Hot Chili Peppers describes the sound of the band's music

CITY OF ORIGIN: Los Angeles, California

CURRENTLY RESIDE IN: Los Angeles area

STYLE OF MUSIC: rock, punk, funk, metal, thrash

AWARDS/NOMINATIONS:

* 1999 Grammy Award Nomination for *Californication*

* 1999 Grammy Award, Best Rock Song, "Scar Tissue"

* 1992 Grammy Award, Best Hard Rock Performance with Vocal, "Give It Away"

* MTV Music Video Awards for *Under the Bridge* and *Give It Away*

Discography:

* Californication (1999)
* Best of Red Hot Chili Peppers (1998)
* One Hot Minute (1995)
* Blood Sugar Sex Magik (1991)
* Mother's Milk (1989)
* The Abbey Road E.P. (1988)
* The Uplift Mofo Party Plan (1987)
* Freaky Styley (1985)
* Red Hot Chili Peppers (1984)

"We all know not to project how many years this thing is going to work," Anthony says about the band's success, "but right now, it's working like crazy."

RANDOM FACTS:

* RHCP toured with the Foo Fighters during the summer of 2000
* Before they were called RCHP the guys called themselves "Tony Flow and the Majestic Masters of Mayhem"
* The guys in the band like to listen to David Bowie, the Cure, and the Germs
* Anthony, Flea, and Chad are all the same age. Their birthdays are within two weeks of each other
* The band is mostly vegetarian, although sometimes they cheat!

OFFICIAL WEBSITE: www.redhotchilipeppers.com

THE BOYS IN THE BAND:

Name: Michael Peter Balzary; aka Flea
Birth date: October 16, 1962
Birthplace: Melbourne, Victoria, Australia
Musical instrument: bass, trumpet
Musical influences: Dizzy Gillespie, Miles Davis

RANDOM FACTS:

* Flea has a daughter named Clara
* Flea is working on a solo project
* Flea loves to cook

QUOTABLE QUOTE:

* "I didn't know anything about rock music [when I started playing guitar]. . . . But before I . . . played, I visualized myself making the bass as exciting as any guitar player, jumping around, going crazy."

Name: Anthony Kiedis
Birth date: November 1, 1962
Birthplace: Grand Rapids, Michigan
Musical instrument: vocals
Musical influences: Sly and the Family Stone, George Clinton

RANDOM FACTS:

* Anthony's nickname is "Antwan the Swan"
* Anthony's favorite sport is swimming

QUOTABLE QUOTE:

* Anthony believes in good luck. One of the first things he ever told Flea when they were in high school: "If a plane crashes, I'm the guy who survives."

Name: John Frusciante
Birth date: March 5, 1970
Birthplace: New York, New York
Musical instrument: guitar
Musical influences: Frank Zappa, Kiss

RANDOM FACTS:

* John was eighteen years old when he joined RHCP
* John was a big fan of RHCP before he joined the band

QUOTABLE QUOTE:

* "At nineteen, I might have looked [strong], but I was a weakling inside. I wasn't proud of who I was then. And now I'm proud of who I am."

Name: Chad Smith
Birth date: October 25, 1962
Birthplace: St. Paul, Minnesota
Musical instrument: drums
Musical influences: Led Zeppelin, The Who, Kiss, Van Halen, Jimi Hendrix

RANDOM FACTS:

* Chad is married to Maria; they have a daughter named Manon
* Chad used to "drum" by banging on Baskin-Robbins containers
* RHCP auditioned thirty drummers before they accepted Chad
* Chad rides a Harley Davidson
* Chad's favorite sports are hockey (he's a Detroit fan) and baseball

QUOTABLE QUOTE:

* Chad was one of the loudest drummers the guys in RHCP had ever heard. He defends the noise by saying, "I could play quiet, but I'm more of the bashing type."

John Frusciante

THE RED HOT STORY

The Red Hot Chili Peppers continue to live up to their name, burning up the charts with the release of their seventh album. This hip party band has been together for eighteen years. During the past two decades RHCP have introduced and developed a style of music that blends punk, thrash, and funk. They paved the way for bands like Sugar Ray and Offspring.

RHCP have changed a lot over the years, band members have come and gone, but there's no doubt about the quality of their latest album — everyone loves it. According to Anthony Kiedis, RHCP lead singer, it's mostly about looking forward to happy things as well as the disappointment of broken promises. Anthony explains that the album is a series of songs "about California and Hollywood having such a [big] effect on the planet . . . of the good and the bad of that. Of how people dream of this weird, magical place that is really kind of the end of the world."

For the band, the album has been nothing but good. The tour in support of it (with Foo Fighters) was a total sell out and they enjoyed the sweet success of being hotter than the summer heat.

HOW TO BE A PEPPER

The road to success has had lots of curves since the band first got together in 1983. It all began at Fairfax High School in Los Angeles. At the age of fifteen Michael Balzary (or, as fans know the band's bass player, Flea) became friends with Anthony Kiedis. The two shared a common bond in that neither was a Los Angeles native. Flea was born in Melbourne, Australia, and lived in New York for a while before his family moved to Los Angeles. Anthony had grown up in Michigan where he lived with his mom before he moved to the West Coast to be with his dad. Both were very much into show business. Flea's dad was a jazz musician, so he'd grown up around music. While Flea was in high school he joined a punk band called Fear. Meanwhile, Anthony wanted to be an actor and was actually having a little luck auditioning for small roles in films and television. At the same time that Flea and Anthony were becoming friends, another of Flea's buds, Hillel Slovak, was teaching himself guitar.

After graduation from high school Flea and Hillel decided to form a band. They called it Another School and asked one of Hillel's best buddies to join them on drums. Jack Irons accepted the invitation — and the band, as a threesome, was complete.

FLEA

Immediately they started playing on the LA club circuit. They recruited wannabe actor Anthony as master of ceremonies. He'd often read one of his poems before the band went onstage. One night Anthony jammed with the guys onstage during their performance and the creative energy between all of them was so hot, he joined the group as their lead singer. Within six months, they were offered their first record contract.

OFF TO A ROCKY START

The band had gotten good enough to record and decided to go into the studio to make their first record. But right before they did, Hillel and Jack quit the band. Anthony and Flea quickly recruited some other musicians and kept the band going. It would not be the first time that the lineup shifted so fast. In fact, there are only two albums in all the RHCP discography that were actually recorded by the band's original lineup.

Despite the setback, RHCP released their first self-titled album in 1984. It didn't sell well. Luckily, Hillel and Jack returned to the band and they continued to do many live performances. Their fan base steadily increased and the name Red Hot Chili Peppers spread around town.

By 1985 the band felt ready to record again and released their second album, *Freaky Styley.* This album was a little more funky than the first one, and again, they performed live to support its sales.

In 1987, RHCP released their third album, *The Uplift Mofo Party Plan,* which was their first record to actually make it onto the charts. Next they put out *The Abbey Road E.P.* — their pose on the cover imitated the famous Beatles pose from an album of the same name. Again, the band went on the road for a long time. When they came home, tragedy struck — Hillel died. And soon, Jack left the band. For a while, RHCP called it quits and all the members went their separate ways. After a while, though, Anthony and Flea decided to get the band back together. They found John Frusciante to play guitar and got Chad Smith to drum.

YOU CAN'T KNOCK THIS BAND DOWN

In good shape musically, the new foursome went into the studio in 1989 and recorded a fourth album, *Mother's Milk.* The songs "Knock Me Down" and "Higher Ground" were big hits and the album became the band's first huge success. Warner Brothers offered RHCP a contract, and they took it. The band immediately began to work on a follow-up album, which they released in 1991. Entitled *Blood Sugar Sex Magik,* this fifth album was the breakout one. "Give It Away" and "Under the Bridge" became fan favorites and it seemed that the band's success was finally secure. Or not.

John Frusciante was not at all happy about RHCP's fame and fortune. "I got it into my head that stardom was something evil. If you were a rock star, you were trying to put people on." Feeling overwhelmed by success and his own feelings about it, John left just before RHCP was scheduled to headline the Lollapalooza tour in the summer of 1992.

RHCP quickly found a replacement and went on the road while John went off to record on his own. Over the next six years many guitarists replaced John, but the one who lasted the longest and recorded the next album with RHCP was Dave Navarro, the former guitarist for Jane's Addiction.

In 1994 RHCP began working on a new album, *One Hot Minute*, which they released the following year. It was a difficult album to make. Dave's method for recording was a laborious process that involved many long hours of working all alone instead of jamming with the band like John did. By the time the record was finished, tensions between band members were very strained and Dave decided to quit.

Clearly, this was not unfamiliar territory for RHCP! Luckily, Flea never lost touch with John and in 1998 he asked John to rejoin the band. John immediately agreed. According to Chad, "The chemistry with the four of us is the best lineup." No one knew whether or not the chemistry would be right the second time around but the guys were willing to give it a try — and it was more than there. Anthony remembers their first reunited rehearsal. "When [John] hit that first chord, it was so perfect — this blend of sounds from these people who I hadn't heard play together in so long." The sound turned out to be more than perfect, it was the beginning of the band's developing new material for their seventh album, which was released in 1999: *Californication* has become the band's biggest hit album so far. "A lot of these songs started as jams," Flea says. "As soon as John came back into the band we jammed in my garage all summer. Then we did the album in three weeks." Actually, the basic tracks were recorded in just five days.

Since the band lives in California it's no big surprise that they would write about their experiences there. One of the album's most interesting acoustic songs is "Road Trippin'," which came out of a surfing trip that Flea, Anthony, and John took together up at Big Sur, which is a popular place in California to catch some waves. Anthony recalls that they drove up the West Coast in Flea's truck planning to ride the surf, but "as soon as we got there, we started a campfire, [John and Flea] started playing, and I started writing. By the end of the day, I had this song about our trip — that we were together after all this time and doing something as [simple] as surfing and writing music."

RHCP may make writing music look easy, but it's been a struggle for this band to get to the top. Each member has had his own personal ups and downs, and as a band, they have come together and called it quits, hired and retired more members than most other successful bands. But Anthony doesn't see any of the tough times as being bad. "If I've learned anything through the [difficult times] of this experience, it's that all of the setbacks, all of the losses and all of the gains — it's all for a reason. . . . things turn out that way they were supposed to." If what was supposed to happen was that after eighteen years RHCP would be on top of the charts and one of the hottest bands in the land, then Anthony was right.

ChAd SMIth

Anthony KIedIs

FLeA

John FrusclAnte

90

CHAPTER 10

EVERLAST

Name: Eric Schrody

Birth date: August 18, 1969

Birthplace: New York, New York

Lives now: Los Angeles, California

Musical influences: Johnny Cash, Neil Young, Miles Davis

Musical instruments: vocals, acoustic guitar

Musical style: rap-rock, hip-hop, blues

Official website: www.everlastlive.com

Everlast's band is White Folx. Members include:

* Keefus — keyboards
* Bron — slide guitar
* Pablo — drums

HOW TO CONTACT:

Everlast, c/o Tommy Boy Records,
902 Broadway, New York, New York 10010

AWARDS/NOMINATIONS:

* 1999 Grammy award for Best Rock Performance by a Duo or Group with Vocal; "Put Your Lights On" with Carlos Santana

RANDOM FACTS:

* Everlast used to be a graffiti artist
* Everlast was a protégé of Ice-T
* Everlast was in the film *Judgment Night* and *A Prince Among Thieves*
* House of Pain was in the film *Who's the Man*

BIGGest Hits:

* "Jump Around" with House of Pain
* "What It's Like"
* "Put Your Lights On" with Santana

Discography:

* *Whitey Ford Sings the Blues* (1998)
* *Truth Crushed to Earth Shall Rise Again* (1996)
* *Same As It Ever Was* (1994)
* *House of Pain* (1992)
* *Forever Everlasting* (1990)

* Everlast has many tattoos covering his forearms, including a boxing leprechaun
* Everlast wears a gold and diamond necklace that spells his name
* *Eating at Whitey's* features such stars as B-Real (Cypress Hill), N'Dea Davenport (The Brand New Heavies), Rahzel (The Roots), Cee-lo (Goodie M.O.B.), and famous musician Beck's father, folk artist David Campbell

QUOTABLE QUOTES:

* Explaining how his outlook has changed over the course of his musical career, Everlast says: "My first record was like not knowing what . . . I was doing. Then House of Pain was like my angst record. . . . To me [*Whitey Ford Sings the Blues*] is art now."

* "I'm playing as much as I can play, and I don't care if there's ten people or ten thousand. So far, I feel it's working. Right now I'm enjoying my music more than I ever have before. I mean, that's all that matters now. I've had [fortune and fame] and none of that ever made me as happy as when I'm making music."

THE EVERLAST STORY

You might not expect an Irish kid from Los Angeles to make it to the top of the hip-hop scene, but if you know Eric Schrody, aka Everlast, you know that's just what he did. One of the only Caucasians in Ice-T's Rhyme Syndicate in the '80s, Everlast found tons of fame as the front man for House of Pain in the '90s. And then he chucked it all to go out on his own and develop a whole new sound.

One of the hallmarks of Everlast's success has been his constant ability and desire to change. Now, with the big success of his second solo album, *Whitey Ford Sings the Blues*, he's changed himself and his sound again. No more straight hip-hop for this rap artist. Instead he has blended the hip-hop beat with a folksy blues rhythm and created a whole new sound — and fans are digging it.

GETTING INTO THE HIP-HOP SCENE

Everlast has had what some would say was an easy trip to the top. Born in New York, he moved to Los Angeles at the age of two when his dad decided to take the family across the country in search of a better job. Everlast was introduced to rap by a friend one summer while they were at camp and he got hooked on writing. He quickly became a "rap prodigy," rhyming and making four-track tapes with fellow hip-hopper Divine Styler. Eventually Everlast recorded a couple of tracks with the help of his friend's DJ partner — and amazingly Ice-T heard the tape. As a matter of fact, Ice-T liked Everlast's talent so much he invited Everlast to join the Rhyme Syndicate. Everlast was only seventeen when he toured the United Kingdom with Ice-T's crew.

Not one to stay in the background for long, Everlast released his first solo album in 1990. It was produced by Ice-T and was called *Forever Everlasting.* Although it was a solid hip-hop effort, it did not bring Everlast any fame; that came two years later when he joined an Irish pride hip-hop band called House of Pain.

EVERLAST IN THE HOUSE

One of the biggest rap groups in the early '90s was House of Pain, a band put together by Everlast with two of his friends from school, Danny "Danny Boy" O'Connor and Leor "DJ Lethal" Dimant. The guys put together a demo that included a recording of "Jump Around" and within weeks they had a record deal. In 1991 they exploded onto the hip-hop scene with the release of their first album, *House of Pain.* Featuring the huge hit "Jump Around," the album reached platinum status. Everlast started living large and having fun, but "it got to the point where all I cared about was the size of the check," he says. Music began to be a business to him, not the pleasure it used to be, not "that thing that puts butterflies in your gut before you go onstage. It got to the point with House of Pain where it was a machine. Get onstage. Do the show. Get off. Go to the hotel. It was too routine. The only reason I was going on the road was to make money. Once I stopped getting butterflies, that's when I knew things were going to get boring." This was the beginning of the end for House of Pain.

The group's next two albums did not do so well as their first, although the second record, *Same As It Ever Was,* did go gold when it was released in 1994. The big songs off that album were "Boom Sha Lock Lock" and "Who's the Man." The band went on tour and then went back into the studio to record their follow-up album, *Truth Crushed to Earth Shall Rise Again,* which was released in 1996.

Unfortunately, by then the band had developed serious internal problems. Everlast and Danny were not getting along. It got so bad that Everlast quit the band the night of the release party for *Truth Crushed to Earth Shall Rise Again.* "That was probably the meanest thing I ever did," he admits. "Because I did it to be mean. And I regret that. We were just about to do 'Jump Around' and I turned around and said, 'Yo, enjoy it, because this is the last time we're doing this.' And then we finished the show and I just walked out." That was the end of House of Pain, but just the beginning of Everlast's new solo career.

PROVING THAT HE CAN OUTLAST ANYTHING

The years 1996 to 2000 were busy ones for Everlast. He completely "reinvented" himself and formed a new identity separate from his rap boy days. First, he spent some time just writing down new ideas. He says that writing "usually comes to me through depression . . . not because I believe it's gotta be that way. But because something always seems to happen before I'm about to write a record." While he writes, he adds, he doesn't listen to any music at all because he's afraid that what he hears will influence him too much and get in the way of his own creativity. To back up his new songs, Everlast found a new band to play with him; White Folx has a keyboardist, a drummer, and a slide guitar.

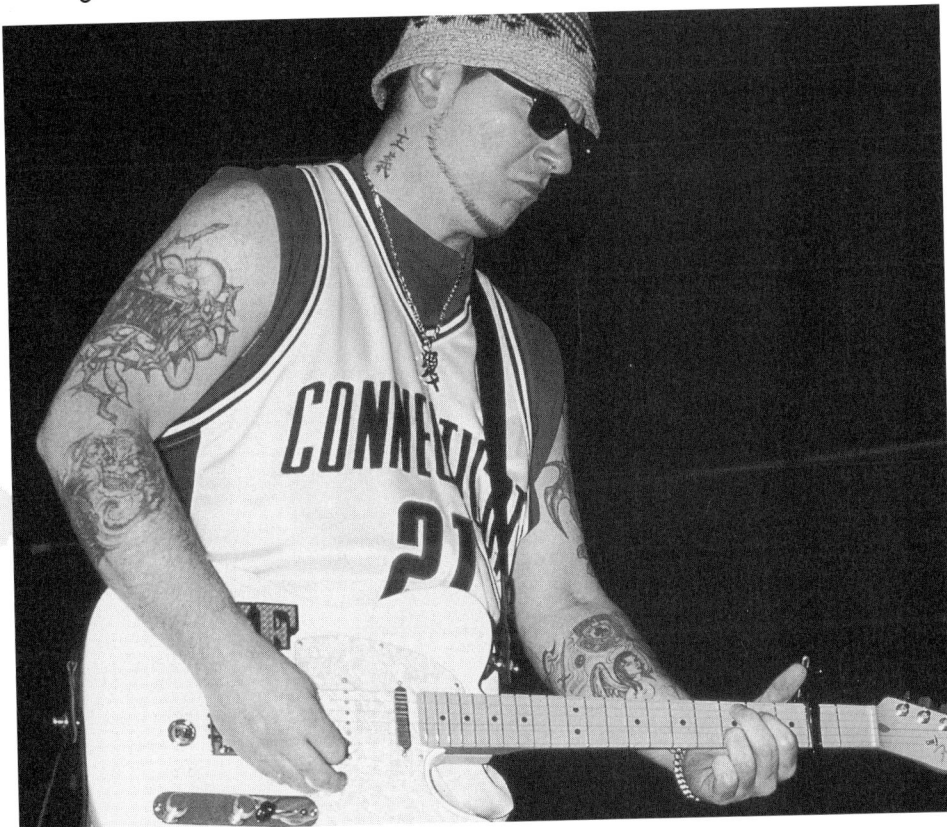

In 1998 Everlast and White Folx went into the studio to record Everlast's second solo album, *Whitey Ford Sings the Blues.* Everlast played guitar on the record and wrote all of the songs. The album is named after a legendary Yankees baseball pitcher and basically tells the story of a man growing up. It has a very different sound from Everlast's previous songs. Instead of hardcore rap, *Whitey* still has its base in rap, but also adds acoustic guitar, plus some country and blues influences. "I had always played guitar," Everlast explains, "but I . . . resisted doing it on a hip-hop record" because he did not think people would accept the combination. Boy, was he wrong!

Whitey was released in 1998 but it didn't really chart until the year 2000, when it became a huge success. The video for "What It's Like" went into heavy rotation on MTV and broke the album out onto the charts. Everlast explains that the album is about empathy, about not judging the person next to you because everyone is equal. Most of the songs are taken from his own experiences, including "The Letter" and "Seven Years," which are about the breakup of his long-term relationship with a girlfriend.

TRANSFORMATION COMPLETE

It's been a long and fast ride from rap fame to acoustic hip-hop artist, but Everlast has hung on despite the ups and downs of professional problems and a serious health scare. In 1998, on the last day of recording the *Whitey* album, Everlast suffered a massive heart attack, which was attributed to a birth defect in his heart. Luckily doctors were able to save him and he has been able to enjoy the success of his solo career. Since the new album was released Everlast was invited to be one of the many stars to perform at Woodstock '99, and he toured with Lenny Kravitz and the Black Crows. A highlight of his recent ride is his musical collaboration with Carlos Santana. The bluesy tune "Put Your Lights On" was one of several fabulous tracks on the Grammy award winning album *Supernatural.*

What's up next for this musical chameleon? "I can't wait to make another record," Everlast says. "I'm just finding a style now. Everything that I thought was limited before weren't limitations, they were just fears. I'm not scared to try [anything anymore]. That's what [*Whitey*] is about, shedding any fears. People are either going to love [the] record or think I've lost my mind. Either one of those is okay with me."